LANGUAGE AND AREA STUDIES
IN THE ARMED SERVICES

COMMISSION ON IMPLICATIONS OF ARMED SERVICES EDUCATIONAL PROGRAMS

Appointed by the American Council on Education

EDMUND E. DAY, Cornell University, *Chairman*

HORACE M. BOND, Lincoln University

HOWARD A. CAMPION, Los Angeles Public Schools

J. WALTER DIETZ, Summit, New Jersey

ANNA L. ROSE HAWKES, Mills College

HENRY H. HILL, George Peabody College

HEROLD C. HUNT, Kansas City (Missouri) Public Schools

T. R. McCONNELL, University of Minnesota

CARL H. MILAM, American Library Association

HARRY S. ROGERS, Brooklyn Polytechnic Institute

GEORGE F. ZOOK, American Council on Education, *ex officio*

ALONZO G. GRACE, *Director*

M. M. CHAMBERS, *Associate Director*

★ Here is a study of the techniques of foreign area and language instruction in the wartime college training programs. The armed services' experience with the teaching of language and area studies stimulated widespread interest and suggested the possibility that American students in civilian schools could attain a speedier and more thorough grasp of foreign languages and, at the same time, acquire a more practical understanding of foreign peoples and their cultures.

To meet wartime demands, the learning of foreign languages in the armed services training programs had to be directed toward sharply defined functional ends. The experiences of these programs suggest that unprecedented speed in acquiring an alien tongue may be attainable. Intensive courses in a planned environment, making wide use of native informants and mechanical recordings, may be the means of encouraging quick mastery of the vernacular and of stimulating and aiding the study of an alien culture.

This report describes in detail foreign area and language instruction in the Army Specialized Training Program, the Navy Schools of Military Government and Administration, the Japanese Language Schools of the Army, and the Civil Affairs Training Schools. It reports modifications in many college programs, includes a chapter on an experiment at secondary level, and points to implications for both language and area studies in American secondary and higher education.

AMERICAN COUNCIL ON EDUCATION

★ The publisher of this volume, the AMERICAN COUNCIL ON EDUCATION, is a council of national educational associations; organizations having related interests; approved universities, colleges, and technological schools; state departments of education; city school systems and private school systems; selected private secondary schools; and selected educational departments of business and industrial companies. The AMERICAN COUNCIL ON EDUCATION operates through a number of committees and commissions composed of outstanding leaders in American education and public life.

The Commission on Implications of Armed Services Educational Programs began its work in July 1945. It undertakes to identify features of the wartime training and educational programs worthy of adaptation and experimentation in peacetime civilian education of any and all types of levels.

744 Jackson Place
Washington, D.C.

LANGUAGE
AND AREA STUDIES
IN THE
ARMED SERVICES

Their Future Significance

BY *Robert John Matthew*

FOR THE COMMISSION ON IMPLICATIONS
OF ARMED SERVICES EDUCATIONAL
PROGRAMS

AMERICAN COUNCIL ON EDUCATION
Washington, D. C.

COPYRIGHT 1947

BY THE AMERICAN COUNCIL ON EDUCATION

PRINTED IN THE UNITED STATES OF AMERICA

FOREWORD

As THIS report was being completed in the autumn of 1946, the "Truculent Turtle" of the United States Navy made its historic nonstop flight from Australia to Ohio, and the "Pacusan Dreamboat" of the Army Air Forces roared over the frozen Arctic from Hawaii to Cairo. A meeting-place on Long Island was being readied for the delegates of the United Nations, who were to come speaking in many tongues.

No more is necessary to emphasize that the shrinking of our "one world" gives doubly renewed importance to the teaching and learning of modern languages and of the cultures of foreign areas. The same point had been forcibly presented during the war, when our armed forces were distributed over much of the habitable globe; and both the Army and the Navy instituted various programs of language and area studies which constitute the subject of this report.

How this instruction was organized and conducted, what it accomplished, and what it may promise for American youth in colleges and schools forms one distinct segment of the general responsibilities of the Commission on Implications of Armed Services Educational Programs. For this investigation the Commission employed Dr. Robert John Matthew, formerly a captain in the Army Air Forces and regularly a member of the staff of the Department of Romance Languages at the College of the City of New York.

In consideration of the importance of his study, Dr. Matthew was given the advice and guidance of a special committee of seven eminent educators in pertinent fields, under the distinguished leadership of Professor Robert Herndon Fife of Columbia University, who was for more than twenty years chairman of the Committee on Modern Languages of the American Council on Education. The special committee, having approved this report, contributes a brief special foreword on a later page.

In common with studies on other aspects of the work of the Commission, this study had the approval of the Secretary of

War and the Secretary of the Navy as to its general purposes, and they facilitated its progress by designating as official liaison agencies respectively the Historical Division of War Department Special Staff and the Standards and Curriculum Division, Training Activity, Bureau of Naval Personnel. These agencies provided full access to documentary materials and to officers formerly in charge of the several language and area programs.

The same agencies also reviewed the study in manuscript, on occasion gave valuable suggestions, and finally approved the draft for factual accuracy and to safeguard information vital to the national security. It is understood, however, that opinions and assertions contained in the report are not to be construed as official or as reflecting the views of the War Department or the Navy Department or of the military or naval services at large.

Dr. Matthew made personal visits to several selected colleges and universities for the double purpose of collecting data on the armed services language and area programs and of studying recent developments in his field. Thus this report has the peculiar advantage of presenting not only what the armed services did in time of war, but also what the civilian institutions are subsequently doing to implement the lessons of wartime training.

ALONZO G. GRACE
Director

FOREWORD BY THE SPECIAL COMMITTEE ON LANGUAGE AND AREA STUDIES

THE COMMITTEE appointed by the Director of the Commission to supervise and sponsor the investigation of implications for civilian education to be derived from the language and area programs of the armed services begs to submit its approval of the following report by Dr. Robert J. Matthew. The committee undertook its task in November 1945 and held three meetings for conference with Dr. Matthew and for consideration of plans and progress, as follows: at Chicago, December 29–30, 1945, for definition of the project and examination of the data already gathered; at Washington, April 6–7, 1946, for consideration of the source material gathered and of plans for its collation and a general outline of the report; at New York, July 27–28, 1946, for criticism of the draft prepared by Dr. Matthew, advice as to its arrangement and revision, and steps toward formulation of conclusions and implications.

In approving the report, the members of the committee are fully aware of the many questions that have to be left unanswered for the present. It has been found possible to assemble a mass of sources covering the directives of the Army and Navy for organization and method, and the results of this investigation have shown themselves adequate for drawing a comprehensive picture of the programs. This alone was a considerable undertaking and could not have been carried out without the cooperation of those in charge of official records, both at headquarters in Washington and in civilian institutions.

On the other hand, actual results obtained at the various centers of instruction could not be measured by any means now at our command. No objective tests to determine the degree of final achievement at the various schools in language competence and areal knowledge were administered so far as we have been able to learn. The wealth of material regarding results of these courses published in the educational and public press, based on the opinion of instructors, students, and observers, or on mere hearsay, is so confused and so often contradictory that it offers no safe basis for categorical statements respecting success in achievement of goals set by the Army and Navy. It is, however, evident that the general character of the results of this tremendous expenditure of energy and cooperative effort has opened new vistas for language and area training in postwar years.

Based on such information as could be gathered, certain general conclusions regarding the application of the programs of the armed services to civilian education in the fields specified are possible, and a formulation of these has been undertaken. It will be noted that many of the statements in the final chapter of this report take the form of questions for which answers have still to be sought. The undersigned committee and the investigator agree that these unsolved problems are in themselves part of the implications to be drawn from the programs prescribed by the Army and Navy for civilian education, and that to make deductions where the premises are incomplete would be only to add to the mass of subjective opinion which clutters educational literature. However, the report seeks to define as precisely as possible the lines which experiment must follow if teachers and administrators are to avoid a waste of time and effort and if the impulse given by the armed forces is to have a lasting effect.

The widespread interest of educationists, subject-matter teachers, and the general public in the Army and Navy courses is a very impressive implication of this wartime effort. The intensive character of the work, the emphasis on oral and aural readiness in languages, the promotion of individual competence in the living language, the necessity for adequate supervision of instruction, an accurate definition of objectives, and the liberal use of realia, while not just exactly innovations, strike the educational world with an impact hitherto unknown. The challenge which they make has already been met by some of the institutions which are seeking to implement their wartime experiences for civilian learners. The Chicago testing project, sketched in chapter ix, is engaged in applying objective tools of measurement to the results of experiments in language instruction in a number of colleges and at least one preparatory school. The data from these and other efforts at implementation are not yet available, and it is hoped that the Commission may find that its mandate permits the continuance of the investigation in the field of language and area study through another year, when lessons can be drawn from efforts to implement the armed services' educational programs and these can be fully studied.

In addition to the present report by Dr. Matthew, the Commission is publishing separately another document, a report of a survey of the foreign-area curriculum of the Army Specialized Training Program and the Civilian Affairs Training Program, prepared by Dr. William N. Fenton. This is the completion of a task which he began during his services as research associate with the wartime Ethnogeographic Board and is based on material gathered by his own visits and those of associates to the area courses when they were in progress in 1943–44. The committee did not have opportunity to examine the report in detail or to weigh conclusions which Dr. Fenton appends. It feels, however, that this account of the effort in area instruction is a proper supplement to the picture drafted through Dr. Matthew's investigation, and it is glad to be able to cite it for the additional light it throws on the educational effort of the armed services.

FREDERICK B. AGARD, University of Chicago
HENRY GRATTAN DOYLE, George Washington University
WILLIAM NELSON FENTON, Smithsonian Institution
ROBERT HERNDON FIFE, Columbia University, *Chairman*
STEPHEN A. FREEMAN, Middlebury College
ERNEST J. SIMMONS, Columbia University
WILLIAM F. TWADDELL, Brown University

PREFACE

THE PRACTICE prevalent in America during World War I
was to frown upon the language and culture of the enemy
and to repudiate anything that pertained to him. In World
War II we, as a nation, adopted a totally different point of view.
Instead of denouncing German, Italian, or Japanese, the languages of the enemy, the various branches of the services
put forth every effort to have their personnel learn them. And,
what is more important, to learn them so well in some instances
as to be able to converse effectively with natives! How this
point of view, this right-about-face attitude, toward the languages
of the enemy nations came about is a phenomenon which we are
not to explain here. Interesting as the psychology behind this
change in outlook is, it does not form a proper part of this study.
Not only were the languages of Germany, Italy, and Japan
studied, but other little-known languages of the Near East and
the Orient as well.

The story of the Army and Navy foreign language and
area programs, which are characterized by the close relationship between area and language, is one of captivating interest.
Whether the motivation or the objectives of the armed services
programs will ever again be so clearly defined for civilian education is doubtful. On the other hand, there is much that can
be learned from the Army and Navy experiences.

From the numerous articles and critical studies by language
teachers on the intensive language courses and the oral approach
to language learning, it is apparent that a new interest has been
awakened. Placing emphasis on an intensive study of one foreign
language and attempting to produce competent speakers of that
language are rare in our schools and colleges. The means by
which this competence was to be achieved—by intensive, accelerated courses, and by use of the oral method—presents an
interesting challenge to civilian education.

The areal program that accompanied the study of the language
and for which the language was to provide a complementary
discipline is also gaining currency in the thinking of those respon-

sible for the planning of new courses of study. Distinct from schools of international studies and interdepartmental majors, integrated area study, which is usually centered about that region where the language is spoken, is defined as the focusing of all the disciplinary competences (such as geography, history, economics, languages and literature, philosophy, and political science) upon a cultural area for the purpose of obtaining a total picture of that area.[1]

The interdepartmental cooperation and the interplay of the various participating disciplines that were characteristic of the several programs in varying degrees offer much for the consideration of civilian educators. The emphasis placed on the contemporaneous scene in the presentation of area study furnishes a new concept in curriculum procedures. Since the value of such a course of study is directly dependent upon the degree to which it achieves the necessary integration, much experimentation will be required and many failures will no doubt be recorded before area study will come into its own.

The programs sponsored by the Army and Navy and described in this report owe their origin in part to theories and practices that existed in the prewar period. For the purpose of the intensive study of languages, emphasizing the oral approach and the use of native speakers—called "informants"—in small drill sessions, the Army took over and developed further a technique which was discovered and practiced by the late Franz Boas, anthropologist of Columbia University, an ardent and original leader of research in the field of the American Indian. Boas, and others who followed him, among them Edward Sapir and Leonard Bloomfield, believed that written documents were at best a very imperfect record of actual speech and that the only sound way to learn to speak a new language is to imitate as exactly as possible what the native speakers say. This was the technique which was adopted in learning the nonliterate languages of some of the American Indian tribes. These scholars were among a group who in 1923 organized themselves as the Lin-

[1] Mortimer Graves, "A Basic Program of Area Studies for the American Council of Learned Societies" (Mimeographed; Washington: American Council of Learned Societies, 1946).

guistic Society of America.   Until almost 1930, their efforts were
confined to scholarly research.   In the late 1930's they began
to apply their new ideas to language instruction and introduced
a number of innovations.   First they insisted that students should
spend most of their learning time in imitating a native speaker.
This was to be done in drill sessions where small groups of
students met with a native speaker or informant and were drilled
on assigned materials.   Secondly, in place of the traditional
course of three or four hours a week, they insisted on at least
fifteen to twenty contact hours a week.   Thirdly, they believed
that the study of grammar should occupy an ancillary place in
the instructional program.   Since the sole aim during the first
stage of language instruction is to help a learner imitate the
speech of a native, grammar should be taught only to the extent
that it can aid this imitative process.   Finally, they believed that
the study of reading and writing should not be allowed to inter-
fere with learning to speak a language.   Where there is a close
correspondence between sound and spelling, and a familiar alpha-
bet is used, reading and writing can be taught from the beginning.
Where this is not the case, it is better to start the student off
with a simplified form of spelling and teach him the traditional
native spelling only when he has acquired considerable control
over the spoken language.

     For area study, there had been less experimentation.   There
were before the war, however, programs in area study at several
universities from which the ASTP area program can be said to
derive.   These were for the most part regional studies of a
nonintensive, nonintegrated type.   These prewar area programs
presented knowledge of a cultural region in terms of competing
academic disciplines, each discipline scheduled separately and in
sequence rather than as an element of an integrated and synthe-
sized course.   It is to the credit of the wartime area programs,
and of those who planned them, that area study was established
on an integrated basis and that it was spread over a wide area
of disciplines covering the contemporaneous scene.   There was,
to be sure, no great attempt to reach far into the past, but enough
of the past was included to make the present intelligible.   The
historical method as such was little used, but the method of the

cultural historian was adapted to a functional contemporaneous approach.

It becomes apparent from this brief outline of prewar language and area instruction that the armed services adopted and developed for their programs certain educational procedures which were practiced in varying degrees before the war. In fact, an enlightening study could be made of the contribution of civilian education to the armed services educational programs. Another way of considering the problem is in the light of the contributions they have made to each other. This is particularly true of the area and language programs.

In the pages that follow, I have attempted to give a picture of the wartime area and language programs of the armed services, and to point out in these experiences certain implications which are pertinent to civilian education. I have also described certain efforts now under way to implement these experiences by courses in imitation of the armed services programs. Though the nature of these civilian adaptations is tentative and experimental, they corroborate and support the belief that the Army and Navy gave a new impetus to area and language study for the postwar period.

In the effort to draw an adequate picture of this wartime undertaking, it has been necessary to examine a great mass of published material. The bibliography appended to the report gives an indication of the powerful reaction of civilian administrators and teachers to the challenge which was offered them.

ACKNOWLEDGMENTS

This report could not have been initiated or completed without the ever-ready assistance of the committee, both individually and collectively. To the Chairman, who has been untiring in his efforts to present the best report possible in the time allotted, the writer owes a debt which he can never hope to repay.

The writer is also much indebted to large numbers of individuals who have given of their time, effort, and advice. Without their assistance the study would have been impossible. The

institutions which were visited by the writer have been treated
anonymously due to the experimental nature of the programs
that were observed. It is impossible, therefore, to list by name
the several members of the staffs at each institution, who gave
advice and counsel (and some of whose classes the writer visited),
for that would nullify the whole attempt at anonymity which it
is desirable to maintain.

Invaluable assistance has been received from Dr. Mortimer
Graves and Dr. J. Milton Cowan of the American Council of
Learned Societies.

Special mention should be made of Dr. Henry D. Collins of
the Smithsonian Institution for revealing the existence of the
reports on *Area Studies in American Universities,* prepared
under the auspices of the now defunct Ethnogeographic Board
of that organization. William N. Fenton who prepared these
reports and who has just completed a special survey report on
Area Studies in American Universities for the Commission has
been most helpful.

In the War Department, to Captains Harold F. Underhill
and Boyd C. Shafer, and to Dr. Walter L. Wright, Chief Historian, special thanks are due for their guidance and help. In
the Navy Department, Captains Bartky, Hindmarsh, and Turn-
bull have rendered invaluable service. Without the assistance of
these officers of the War and Navy departments, the channels
of investigation would have remained closed and excellent source
material would have been unavailable.

Professor George E. Taylor of the University of Washington,
and Professor Robert Hall of the University of Michigan have
offered valuable suggestions.

To Dr. Theodore Huebener, director of foreign languages
for New York City, the writer is especially grateful. He accepted unhesitatingly the challenge of furthering an experiment
in language teaching on the secondary level for the Commission.
It is from his summary of the experiment that the section relating
to the secondary schools is taken.

ROBERT JOHN MATTHEW

Washington, D. C.
January 1947

CONTENTS

Part One: What the Armed Services Did

Part Two: Current Effects in Colleges and Schools

CONTENTS xix

PAGE

IX. THE UNIVERSITY OF CHICAGO LANGUAGE INVESTIGATION .. 145

    Testing Program 145

    Other Aims of the Investigation 148

X. AREA-STUDY PROGRAMS IN CIVILIAN INSTITUTIONS 149

    Area-study Programs in Operation 151

    Future Plans for Area Study 161

Part Three: Significance for the Future

XI. CONCLUSIONS AND IMPLICATIONS 165

    Language Study 167

    Area Study 172

APPENDIXES

A. INSTITUTIONS OFFERING ASTP AREA AND LANGUAGE INSTRUC-
TION 177

B. FOREIGN AREA AND LANGUAGE CURRICULA 179

C. SUMMARY OF ASTP DEMANDS 186

D. SUMMARY OF ASTP PRODUCTION REPORTS 187

BIBLIOGRAPHY

    General References 188

    Army and Navy Documents 210

Part One

WHAT THE ARMED SERVICES DID

I. GENERAL SURVEY OF LANGUAGE AND AREA PROGRAMS OF THE ARMED SERVICES

A NATION GEARED to the pursuits of war, involving the entire population—men, women, and children—requires vast changes from normal peacetime habits, not only in outlook, but in actual demonstrated practice. The schools, the colleges, and the universities had their share of change, as did industry, business, and the professions. Each had a vital part to play in the shifting programs that were demanded by the War and Navy departments in the prosecution of the war.

The area and language program of the armed services was, to be sure, one of the lesser programs in point of numbers involved, but one which gained tremendous publicity—in fact, more publicity than any other educational phase. The various programs in area and language study were located in colleges and universities throughout the country, and since they were generally designed for similar purposes, they can be considered as being more or less interrelated.

BACKGROUNDS OF THE PROGRAMS

Early in the war—in fact, before Pearl Harbor—the armed services were aware of the need for men with a working knowledge of the languages and peoples of many regions into which it was possible that the course of the war would take them. Men so trained would be needed in the Office of Naval Intelligence in Washington, on duty at naval stations in the Pacific or on isolated ships scattered across the Pacific, and in the Army Air Forces, the Military Intelligence Service, the Provost Marshal General's Office, the Signal Corps, and in all arms of the Army Ground Forces. To satisfy the needs of these various services, the Navy Oriental Language School (discussed in chapter ii) was established at Boulder, Colorado, with an overflow at Stillwater, Oklahoma, and the Foreign Area and Language Program was created by the Army as a major part of the Advanced Phase

Curricula of the Army Specialized Training Program. Languages were also a part of the curriculum of the Military Government School at Charlottesville, Virginia, the Navy School of Military Government and Administration at Columbia, and the Civil Affairs Training Schools. The Military Intelligence School and the Army Japanese Language School at the University of Michigan had their own special programs with more limited objectives. The common objectives of the schools of the various services were that the officers and men be able to speak and understand a foreign language, know the area in which the language is used, and in general have an understanding of the conditions within a given country which might conceivably favor or endanger relations between the services and the people whom they were to govern or in whose midst they were to live, temporarily at least, whether it be enemy-occupied territory or that under allied control.

The world-wide scale on which this enterprise was established is best shown by an enumeration of the languages that were studied, especially if one bears in mind the related area program which was to accompany the study of the language. These languages, some of which had never been taught before in American universities, were: Annamese, Arabic (Moroccan, Syrian), Bengali, Bulgarian, Burmese, Chinese (Cantonese, Foochow, Fukien, Mandarin), Czech, Dutch, Finnish, French, German, Greek, Hindustani, Hungarian, Italian, Japanese, Korean, Malayan, Norwegian, Persian, Polish, Portuguese, Russian, Serbo-Croatian, Spanish, Swedish, Thai, and Turkish. Area study, as the Army envisaged it, was practically a new venture, especially with the emphasis placed on teaching the purely contemporaneous aspect of the region under examination.

The origin of these programs, for the Army, is traceable to the Office of the Provost Marshal General and the Military Intelligence Division, and for the Navy, to the Office of Naval Intelligence and Columbia University. The Military Government Division laid the ground for an area and language curriculum in the Army Specialized Training Program and later in the Civil Affairs Training Schools. Columbia University planned a curriculum in overseas government and administration which was accepted and adopted by the Navy.

Shortly after Pearl Harbor, both the Army and the Navy realized that many officers and enlisted men would be required to handle the delicate problems of military government in occupied territory. Personnel would be required to take over control of the conquered territory immediately after the Army or Navy landed, and further personnel, possibly civilian, would be needed to continue this control after the armed forces had moved on to further conquests.

In general, it was understood that the Army would have jurisdiction in large land areas, such as Japan itself, and the Navy would have control in the islands of the Pacific. This difference in control and in military government interests of the two main arms of the service explains in large measure the essential characteristics of the respective schools that were eventually established. The Navy was then, for the most part, to concern itself with training personnel who would organize local governments in the numerous islands over the vast stretches of the Pacific, where they would have to deal primarily with primitive peoples. The Army, on the other hand, would concern itself with training personnel who would eventually provide temporary military governments in large land areas, in Europe for example, where cultural patterns similar to our own are encountered. Actually the Army established training programs for both Europe and Asia.

The military government schools that were established—the Navy School of Military Government and Administration, the Military Government School at Charlottesville, the Civil Affairs Training Schools, the Company Officers School, first at Fort Oglethorpe, Georgia, and later at Fort Custer, Michigan—had somewhat similar programs both in training with respect to military tactics and military government, and in the more or less academic studies that were established to complement the military side of the training. In addition to the courses concerning basic military training, there were courses on the international law of military government, public administration, labor, police functions in military government, military courts, economics and finance, peoples and customs, tropical sanitation, public health and hygiene, and all the related topics involved in the general welfare of the people to be governed with respect to feeding, housing, clothing, and handling of displaced persons, prisoners, and enemy nationals who might be found seeking protection there. The language of the territory to be governed must also be studied and learned. Not only was it desired that the officers and men be competent speakers of the language, but they were to be able to understand it as spoken by the natives. Such were the curricular interests of the respective schools primarily concerned with military government.

The schools mentioned above, however, were concerned principally with training officers who would actually be responsible for meeting whatever situations should arise, and who would be ultimately responsible for the solution of the problems encountered. It was believed that in addition to this special group of men, a larger group would be required of nonofficer rank, who would assist them in their tasks. For this larger group the Foreign Area and Language Program of the ASTP was created.[1]

The Navy Japanese Language School (later known as the Navy Oriental Language School) and the Army Japanese Language School were established early in the war to provide initially a number of persons competent in Japanese to be used in any general situation where that language was essential. Later, in the Navy school, other oriental languages were added. The primary need for these trainees was in work of an intelligence nature, such as translating captured Japanese documents, broadcasting in Japanese, intercepting Japanese messages, interrogating prisoners of war, and interpreting. In this capacity, they served a special need not general to the armed services.

Though the Foreign Area and Language Program of the ASTP was originally requested by the Provost Marshal General's Office and the curriculum was first adapted to meet that office's requirements, it developed later that all branches of the services were making demands on the Army Specialized Training Division to suit their respective needs. The program, except for slight

[1] For a list of schools offering an area and language curriculum, see Appendix A, p. 177.

changes, remained, however, much the same throughout its brief existence.

SPECIAL FEATURES OF THE PROGRAMS

Certain features which are characteristic of the programs generally are presented in brief form as part of the preliminary survey.

Methods of teaching

The chief interest of the language training of the wartime programs described in this report concerns the oral skills. Emphasis was placed on teaching the trainee to speak the language "fluently, accurately, and with an acceptable approximation to a native pronunciation." The objective also implied that "the student will have a practically perfect auditory comprehension of the language as spoken by natives." To achieve these ends, intensive courses were established requiring fifteen to eighteen contact hours per week. The courses were handled, in the case of the Army, by senior instructors and informants or drill-masters who were speakers of the language. Large sections were organized for instruction in the structure of the language by the senior instructor, and smaller sections of eight to ten were organized for drill sessions where the language was to be in use at all times. The Navy school did not use the "informant method" but trained its teachers to give all classroom instruction without the aid of "linguists." In some cases the student-teacher ratio was as low as one to two or three, as in the Navy Oriental Language School. Most of the learning was done by mimicry-memorization based on conversational scripts, which were handled by the drill-masters.

The drill sessions were so arranged that the students were forced to take a more active part in the classroom exercises than is normally true for the traditional language class. After the drill-master had recited or read the script a sufficient number of times, the students would be divided into two groups of four to five each and would rehearse with each other the material at hand. Later they would be divided into five groups of two each and again would converse with one another, still repeating the material for the day. This practice was followed in several institutions. The rehearsal of a small amount of subject matter, the grammar for which had been presented earlier by the senior instructor, was first undertaken by the drill-master and later taken up by the small group of students themselves—a method that was largely responsible for the success that was attained in some cases. That the courses were intensive and were limited to language study, with area study complementing the language study, is further reason for their apparent success.

There was some rotation of teachers, periodically scheduled, so that the students were subjected to a wide variety of speech habits and intonations, as well as to different teacher personalities. Supervision of the course was the task of the senior instructor, and the drill-masters were present as observers in the classes where the presentation of grammar took place. When this type of observation and supervision was an integral part of the curriculum, the program was nearly always better.

For the Navy Oriental Language School, examinations were completely divorced from the classroom and were given at special periods not a part of classroom time. Teachers who were chosen to prepare the examinations, to supervise their administration, and to correct them were not always the teachers who taught the students taking the examinations. Sometimes they were not even the teachers who had taught the material upon which the examinations were based.

Writing played a very small part in the total program. For the Army and Navy Japanese language schools, more writing was done than in the ASTP language classes. Some reading was done in the ASTP classes in connection with the attempts to relate area study to language, and vice versa, while in the Navy school it was the reading lesson which served as a basis for both writing and conversing.

In-service training of instructors

A special teacher-training program was a vital part of the Navy language school inasmuch as some of the instructors chosen were not experienced or qualified teachers. They merely knew the language. This training was furthered by weekly faculty seminars, when the faculty assembled for sharing their experiences. Also in the ASTP Foreign Area and Language Program some teacher-training was characteristic of the programs since many refugees and a few trainees were selected to act as drillmasters. The observation required of these teachers in the grammar-presentation classes can be considered as an attempt at a mild form of training while on the job.

Teaching devices: aids to teachers and students

The language and area programs were supplemented in varying degrees, depending upon facilities available and the locality of the institution, by the use of numerous training aids, audio and visual. This was carried out on a much wider scale than is normally the case for civilian education. The Army and the Navy called upon all branches of the government, as well as private industry, to assist in locating and making available a great number of mechanical devices and much specially prepared material.

Many institutions obtained films in considerable numbers for local use. Many more asked the Army Specialized Training Division to furnish them for both language and area instruction, and the Army undertook a considerable survey to secure them. Some of these were made available through the Office of Strategic Services, the Office of Alien Property Custodian, the Museum of Modern Art in New York City, the Provost Marshal General's Office, and the Army Pictorial Service.

Maps in considerable number and variety were distributed by the Army Map Service.

Federal Communications Commission reports containing weekly summaries of foreign broadcasts covering the various theaters of operation and March of Time recordings were also secured and distributed. Because of their timeliness and their general relationship to topics under discussion, these were helpful to the more advanced students who could understand the language.

Civil Affairs handbooks, pocket guides, and language guides were also made available. A great amount of mimeographed and printed language-teaching material was prepared for the

Army Specialized Training Division by the Intensive Language Program sponsored by the American Council of Learned Societies which worked in close collaboration with the ASTD.

Extensive use was made of the phonograph for both listening and recording. The recordings that were made to accompany the language guides and the basic language texts were supplied in large quantities. These were considered an improvement over the usual recording sets because they were provided with pauses during which the students could repeat immediately the recorded matter. Such a device carries the student beyond mere passive listening, and as such was a valuable aid to the teacher. Recordings were made of the lesson materials by the drill-master for study and repeated aural review. Some slight use was made of the radio and the telephone, since in the foreign territory the trainees would be confronted with situations where broadcasts would have to be audited, and the telephone would become the main device for oral communication.

Departmental reorganization and interdepartmental cooperation

On every campus where there was a foreign area and language program a great deal of reorganization of the existing academic disciplines and the faculty in charge of them was necessary before the program was actually set in motion. Both language and area study were under a single coordinator at each institution, and here, perhaps for the first time, the several languages in the Army program were taught by the same method. The coordinator was in charge of the directors of the several courses and was responsible for the scheduling of classes and examinations and the integration of the work in area with the work in language instruction. Frequent class visits and observations by the coordinators and the directors, often unannounced, were the rule. For area study, a special faculty group was designated to plan the details of the program. Faculty members from widely scattered academic disciplines, such as language, anthropology, political science, history, economics, geography, and others, were required to assist in the planning and later to instruct in the program. This required a very marked degree of interdepartmental cooperation not normally conspicuous in academic circles.

In some cases faculty members were actually assigned to deliver lectures they would not voluntarily have given under civilian conditions. Often prepared lectures were submitted for review to the director of a given program or his committee and were revised before delivery to avoid duplication in the program.

Clarity of objective

The objectives of the wartime language and area programs were limited objectives, but they were also clear and precise. The methods employed were related to the attainment of the defined objective. For the Navy, exactly how much should be taught in the allotted time was determined, as well as the exact nature, amount, and sequence of the subject matter to be covered. The techniques were adopted by both the Army and Navy for teaching specifically what was desired. The exercise of close and continued control over the programs was an additional factor that made for attainment of the prescribed objective.

Planning textbook materials

Since teaching materials for many of the languages were non-existent, it was necessary to prepare these on a day-by-day basis. Even in those cases where textbooks were available for the more commonly taught languages, a great deal of new material had to be prepared that was specifically directed to the oral approach. These texts were then used and were improved upon as they came into actual service in the classroom. Progressive revision of the materials used in the classroom meant that unworkable features were recognized and could be omitted in practice.

Supervision of instruction

Close supervision over the individual instructors was constantly maintained in some of the programs for attainment of the objectives and improvement of the instruction. Frequent faculty seminars were held to assure that all participants would benefit by the others' experience. Observations were necessary in a carefully integrated program such as area study in order to avoid duplication of effort and repetition of subject matter presented in the cooperating disciplines.

Planned environment

The idea of a planned environment was not new in language study, since foreign-language houses which are a form of planned environment have long been in existence. These are more generally present in programs of the summer sessions. With the quartering of trainees by the Army and Navy by language groups, and the insistence on use of the foreign language at table and for all outside activities, and with the entire personnel and physical plant—faculty, students, library, and so on—focused on one object, namely, teaching and acquiring a new language, we have perhaps the extensive and complete adoption of what is meant by a planned environment.

Linguists in rare languages and specialists in world regions

Many new languages were taught for the first time in American institutions of higher learning. In these so-called "exotic languages," such as Japanese, Chinese, Malay, and Siamese, a lack of qualified personnel was revealed. This was also true for area study. The wartime programs were able to enlist a large number of foreigners, usually refugees, who were able to assist in these programs and, regardless of their qualifications or training as teachers, their assistance was accepted.

Language learning directed toward functional ends

The Army and Navy language programs were established to train personnel for immediate use of the language in the areas to which they would ultimately be assigned. In so far as the results were successful, they are traceable in large measure to this type of motivation.

Establishment of short intensive courses

Due to the exigencies of the war, the Army and the Navy established numerous short-term, intensive courses to train personnel to perform specific tasks. Many of these, of course, were of a technical nature. There were others, like the Civil Affairs Training Schools program and the Navy School of Military Government and Administration, which established curricula related to the more formal courses of the traditional educational program. These short-term, intensive courses including language and area were planned to qualify personnel for foreign assignment. Refresher courses also were provided for some of the trainees who had already studied a language.

Measurement of results

In most of the training programs of the armed services, the real test of whether or not an individual trainee had received the proper and requisite training rested upon his ability to perform the task for which he was trained. It appears certain that some of the trainees of the language and area programs were able to fulfill their duties satisfactorily in the areas to which they were assigned and were able to cope with the foreign language; that is, they could speak it well enough to be understood and could understand it when spoken. There is little if any objective data available to substantiate the many claims that have been made of the success of the courses. Furthermore, we have no data which give us any convincing information as to whether or not material learned quickly over a short period of time has the same qualities of retention and durability as knowledge acquired over a more extensive period. Until such time as reliable, objective statistics are available regarding these problems, we must rest content with the purely subjective opinions that are advanced by those who advocate the continuance of the wartime methodologies in foreign-language teaching.

II. THE NAVY JAPANESE
LANGUAGE SCHOOL

THE JAPANESE LANGUAGE School sponsored by the Navy, which was later to become the Oriental Language School, was one of the first language schools of the armed services in operation.[1] Long before the war, the United States Navy had been aware of the serious problem which the Japanese language presented to Americans in general, among whom the language was a real enigma except to a few specialists. In December 1940, the Navy was seriously concerned over the small number of naval personnel whom it could count upon as qualified to use the Japanese language. As of that date only twelve officers in the entire Navy of some 200,000 personnel were regarded as fully competent in the use of spoken and written Japanese. When it was learned that only this small number of men were qualified to handle the Japanese language and the proper authorities were advised of this situation, steps were taken at once to try to remedy it.

In addition to the revelation noted above, the Office of Naval Intelligence did not have an up-to-date list of civilians in the United States who were competent and who could be drawn upon in case of an emergency. Before the war only five or six universities were teaching Japanese, and these were not producing qualified linguists who could speak, write, and understand the language. This was indeed an ominous situation confronting the Navy Department which had a right to assume that, in the event of war with Japan, the Navy would be called upon to play a major role in Pacific operations.

The Navy, now fully aware of its impending needs, authorized that a survey of civilians with a workable knowledge of Japa-

[1] This chapter is based primarily on the following documents: Joseph Axelrod, "The Navy Language School Program and Foreign Languages in Schools and Colleges: Aims and Techniques," *Modern Language Journal*, XXIX (January 1945), 40–47; Axelrod, "The Navy Language School and College Foreign Language Departments: Personnel and Organization," *Modern Language Journal*, XXIX (February 1945), 127–32; and Office of the Chief of Naval Operations, *School of Oriental Languages* (MS on file in Office of Naval History, U.S. Navy Department).

nese be made and that steps be taken to organize special training courses in Japanese for naval personnel. It was generally
agreed that these courses should be designed to produce junior
Naval Reserve officers, thoroughly competent in reading, writing, and speaking Japanese, in sufficient numbers to satisfy the
demands which might be made upon the service in the event
of war between Japan and the United States.

One of the first steps taken was to make a nation-wide survey
of all available persons who claimed to know the language,
both in and out of the naval service, with the idea of establishing in the United States a practical course in the Japanese
language.

Between March and June 1941, the Navy built up a file of
600 persons in the United States who were supposed to have
a knowledge of Japanese or Chinese. Of these, 300 possessed
so little knowledge of either language that they were immediately weeded out. Of the remainder, only 56 were selected as
having a background knowledge of Japanese sufficient to warrant
further training. These 56 civilians, all United States citizens
with university degrees, between twenty and thirty-five years of
age, were invited to become the nucleus of the first Navy Japanese Language School. Most of them had lived and studied in
Japan or China.

The next step concerned the selection of a suitable location for
the school and the securing of a competent teaching staff. For
lack of suitable facilities and the requisite curriculum in the
various colleges and universities where Japanese and Chinese
were taught, the Navy decided to set up its own curriculum.
This was a more or less shocking challenge to the traditional
teaching methods in two training centers, Harvard University
and the University of California. It was here that the original
56 men, selected because of their background and knowledge of
Japanese, would be required to take an intensive course of one
year to qualify them as translators and interpreters. The students would enter as civilians, and as soon as practical, after
about a month, would be inducted as Yeomen Second Class, V-4,
USNR, and be placed on active duty. After successful completion of the course, they would be commissioned as officers.

A further real problem which had to be overcome was the scantiness of teaching materials and the evident inadequacies of those available. The Navy decided to adopt the Japanese language readers which had been specially prepared by Naoe Naganuma for the handful of American language officers who came to him for instruction each year in Tokyo. These readers were to serve as the basis of the new intensive course. A supply of these books was received from Japan in September 1941, and they were immediately duplicated in sufficient quantities and made available for the beginning of the first course on October 1, 1941.

There is a particular relationship between Naganuma, his Japanese school in Tokyo, and his prepared texts. Out of his language program sprang the early Naval Japanese Language School. Ever since 1922, the Navy had sent regular officers to Tokyo as Japanese language officers to study the language. This course normally took three years. In these early days, instruction was more or less casual, since each officer was given a special allowance for this purpose and was told to find his own teacher. It was only natural for some students to work as little as they could and to seek, accordingly, teachers who were not too forceful or insistent upon increasingly good and progressive results. Naoe Naganuma, however, was one teacher so highly praised by a number of students that he was soon, about 1925, teaching all the Navy officers. He made the teaching of Japanese to mature men a profession, and he studied this profession scientifically. Soon he began to organize his materials and grade them. Having secured assistant teachers whom he had trained, he finally published, in 1929, the first three volumes of his course. These later were expanded into seven volumes for the full three-year course. They were called *Hyojun Nihongo Tokuhon,* or *Standard Japanese Readers.*

By 1937, Naganuma had trained a staff of fifteen teachers in his methods and materials, and he had an office in the basement of the American Embassy in Tokyo. The Navy financed the printing of his books and guaranteed him a steady income. His texts were never sold. As he gave them only to paying students with the understanding that they were not transferable, the general public was not aware of their existence, and the books were not available for general use. When Naganuma had become president of the Japanese Education Department to spread the Japanese language in Greater East Asia from Manchuria to the Netherlands East Indies, in 1942, the Navy Department had already secured fifty sets of the course for use in its own program in September 1941, having earlier used a master copy which it had in its possession to reproduce in quantity. In 1942 the University of California Press began printing sets, and now all seven volumes plus the accompanying workbooks are on sale to the public.

The Naganuma course normally required three years to complete under conditions in Tokyo, where students had ample opportunity to hear and practice the language with Naganuma's highly trained teachers. The Navy proposed to give the same course in twelve months in the United States, and with teachers yet to be trained. Actually, the first class completed these materials in nine months. The reduction in time with the same program-load was effected by certain calculations followed more or less ruthlessly: by intensive study and teaching, by a high standard of selection of students, and by steadfastly rejecting any procedure which did not adapt itself to the needs and objectives of the school. A list of the texts and other special materials given each student in the course will be found at the end of this chapter.

Of the fifty-six originally selected students, twenty-one were assigned to the University of California and twenty-seven to Harvard, as a result of personal interviews, which came to be the general procedure of selection of all students for this program.

It was believed by the Navy that the student pursuing this course based upon five of the Naganuma language readers together with other specially prepared materials, for twelve months, would be able to read with ease a Japanese newspaper, to converse in Japanese with some degree of fluency, and to handle the language in both its written and spoken form with relative ease and facility. At the end of the course the student was expected to read and write approximately 1,800 to 2,000

Japanese characters and to have a spoken vocabulary of about 7,000 to 8,000 words, with concentration upon what the Navy termed the basic Japanese language, a specialized vocabulary of military and naval terms to be presented to the student after he had acquired with some degree of mastery the so-called basic language. Such were, in general, the broad aims of the Navy Japanese Language School, located at Boulder, Colorado, with an overflow center at Stillwater, Oklahoma.[2]

The specific objectives, classroom procedures, physical conditions governing the course, and the methods used present another picture. The Navy's school objective was fourfold: speaking, understanding, reading, and writing.

READING

It was the reading lesson which served as a basis for writing and conversing as well. Eighteen hours were spent in the classroom per week, of which eight were devoted primarily to reading. Each reading section had a principal reading instructor with whom it met on alternate days for three two-hour periods, and a second reading instructor with whom it met on the two intervening days for a one-hour period. The reading program which included only intensive reading—no extensive reading was involved —was determined in advance by the school director, and all teachers were required to follow this program to the letter.

The work of the first week was primarily oral, but actual study of texts in Japanese characters (including ideographs) was begun at the beginning of the second week after eighteen hours of instruction. The reader and the accompanying workbooks supplied the vocabulary for each lesson, exercises, and brief grammatical explanations. The reader was strictly a reader and did not contain any listed vocabulary as such, or notes, or explanations of any kind, as is true for the usual reading text. It did, however, attempt to introduce vocabulary items, kanji (Japanese characters), and grammatical constructions systematically.

The instructor would normally read a sentence, translate

[2] In June 1942 the Navy school at the University of California was moved to Boulder, Colorado, for security reasons. The Navy's contract with Harvard University expired in September 1942 and was not renewed.

it, and explain grammatical constructions only for the purpose of making clear the meaning of the passage. Students would then be required in turn to repeat the procedure, going through the material as many times as was possible during the hour. Mistakes in pronunciation would be corrected, but no attempt was made to teach the sounds or inflections from the point of view of phonetics. The sounds were learned for the most part by mimicry and memorization. During the reading lessons, Japanese became the medium for routine commands.

It was characteristic of the school that its approach to grammar was nonanalytical. In fact, there was a definite attempt to minimize grammar, syntax, phonetics, linguistics, philology, morphology, and all theory relating to the study of language. Under such a system, students would memorize from the text the sentences which best illustrated the grammatical constructions, once they had understood them, and this they found to be more effective than to attempt to analyze in detail the component parts of the construction. Thus grammar was taught inductively.

WRITING

After each student had mastered the reading lesson, he was required to write out the exercises based on it in the workbook. The exercises were of two types: Japanese to Japanese, answering questions or completing exercises; and English to Japanese, translation into the foreign language. This written work was turned in to the principal reading instructor, who corrected and returned it. The papers were never used as a basis for a planned class activity, probably because in an intensive course of this kind every item was geared for execution in terms of a time limit. However, five hours weekly were devoted to dictation. It was in this class that the students gained facility in writing the characters of the syllabary and the ideographs. With every student at the blackboard, the instructor would begin by dictating the reading lesson of the preceding day, adding, if time permitted, variations by composing sentences involving previously learned vocabulary and constructions. Writing began the first day, utilizing a phonetic *kana* orthography which was to be found in the text and which the instructors used instead of the traditional *kana* orthography. As in the reading class, routine commands were given in Japanese, and after the third week Japanese was used exclusively in all classes.

CONVERSATION

For both the reading and writing classes, especially those classes in which dictation was given, there was, of course, a great deal of aural-oral work. In the conversation class, which met five hours weekly, this oral-aural aim was paramount. Here, the reading lesson of the preceding day was the basis of conversation. Every student was provided with two sets of sentences in *romaji* (Latin characters) with English translation. The first group of sentences consisted of those which dealt primarily with grammatical problems, since they were model sentences, while the second set dealt primarily with actual life situations, such as greetings, travel, or shopping, easily adapted to the conversational approach. Considerable drill was placed on this type of material in endless repetitions varying with the ingenuity of the teacher to introduce variety of arrangement and choice of vocabulary and sentence structure. At no time was pronunciation treated scientifically, that is, no attempt was made to classify the sounds of Japanese, to analyze their production, to show how they differed from or were related to English sounds, or to study the pitch, accent, and tonal inflection. Students had to acquire the sounds and inflections by imitation of the teachers, who were constantly being moved about by a prearranged system of rotation.

A large part of the reader and of the conversation sentences had been recorded and were available to the student for private study in his room. In addition to the phonograph records, a full-length Japanese film made in Japan for commercial use was shown every week, and attendance was required. The same use was made of films in the Russian and Chinese courses. For these films, there were no English titles, but there were brief summaries given in both Japanese and English before the film was shown.

The total time spent by students in this program was incomparably higher than that in any traditional college program. The student worked fourteen hours a day, six days a week, fifty weeks per year. Nine to ten hours a day of this total time were spent in individual study. Examinations, four hours a week, came every Saturday morning, based on the preceding week's coverage.

The students selected for these programs did not all have language backgrounds, but many of them did. Many had had previous training in Chinese and Japanese. Attempts were made, when possible, to place students of similar background in the same sections in the initial stages of the course, and thereafter on the basis of examination grades. Sections were revised so that students of identical capacity could be grouped together. As these students were being paid to study, they cannot be considered students in the usual acceptance of the term. In contrast to the regular student who enters college for any number of reasons, as well as to learn, the students of the Navy Language School knew that they had to learn the language or be dismissed from the school, the consequence of which in time of war meant probable return to civilian status to be immediately picked up by the Selective Service system and to be drafted as a mere private in the Army or an ordinary seaman in the Navy. Outside activities were reduced to the minimum, for the Navy tried to provide for the students ideal working and living conditions: single rooms, if possible, or at most, double quarters; no distractions; no reviews, no parades, no drills, no extraneous military or naval subjects; and only one hour daily of physical exercise.

The director of the school was a Caucasian, but the teaching faculty was primarily made up of first- or second-generation Japanese-Americans with only a few Caucasian instructors. The men and women chosen were not merely informants or drillmasters; they were full-fledged instructors. Many Nisei could not qualify even though they had an excellent command of colloquial spoken Japanese, for anyone who could not handle reading and writing, an integral part of the course, was unsuited for the task. Many of the men and women, while they knew the language from several angles—speaking, writing, grammar, etc.—

had had no previous training in teaching and had not learned the language from the point of view of teaching it, which requires a close linguistic analysis of it. Consequently, attempts were made to fill these gaps by a special teacher-training program and by weekly faculty seminars.

. The centralized system called for an alternation and frequent change of instructors. Each section had, during a period of two months, approximately six different instructors and sometimes more. At the end of this two-month period, a complete shift was made, so that during an entire course students may have had as many as twenty or thirty different instructors. The benefits to- be derived from this type of instruction are many. All students benefit by the best instructors, for it must be assumed that in any educational situation some teachers will be better than others; they are exposed to different teacher personalities; and they profit by contact with the language of different instructors, native and American, men and women, thus being exposed to a variety of intonations.

With a centralized program and centralized examinations, this alternation of instructors is a possibility with no great loss accruing as far as the students are concerned. The Navy school program was carefully planned, all sections covering the same material at the same time and in the same order. The course plans were worked out to the exact number of pages of text to be covered during each class hour. Close control was consequently to be maintained over the entire program. Once the hourly program had been decided upon, every instructor was expected to follow the program faithfully and to the letter. The directors were accustomed to visiting classes frequently and unannounced to observe what was in progress and see that schedules were being maintained.

The examinations at the Navy school were completely divorced from the classroom and were given at special periods not a part of classroom time. They were not necessarily under supervision of any special teachers who might possibly favor this student or that, nor were they always corrected by the same group of teachers. The examinations were for the most part the old-type translations from and into the foreign language. They were made out and graded by an examining committee of instructors which changed from week to week, and they did not necessarily include any of the teachers who had taught the week's work. Oral examinations, in which each student appeared for fifteen minutes before a committee of three instructors, were also given frequently.

Another interesting feature of the Navy language school was the idea of a planned environment, which became a possibility when the school moved to Boulder where it had the status, more or less, of a separate unit. According to reports, the school was a complete functioning unit on its own, merely located at Boulder and using the University of Colorado facilities in conjunction with its own. Thus, the entire institution—students, faculty, equipment, mess hall, entertainment, library, periodicals, radios, and so on—could be focused on one point, namely, learning the language. To this end, the students were required to use the language outside the classroom at all times. The meals were planned about a Japanese setting at least once a day, and instructors mingled with the students at meal time. There were Japanese waitresses, Japanese movies for entertainment, Japanese language used in student newspapers; the school songs were in Japanese; there were Japanese radio broadcasts daily; and as much as possible all campus talk, orders, notices, bulletins, and even outside readings were in Japanese. Each student was provided with phonograph records in Japanese, and since he had a room by himself, he could listen to the language at any hour of the day or night.

The students were treated as college graduates—which most of them were—mature, conscientious, serious, single-minded, bent on one purpose—learning the language. The administration was unrelenting in weeding out the poor students who failed to meet the requirements, regardless of status—civilian, enlisted, or commissioned—regardless of time, whether in the first month or the last, and regardless of effort. The administration was interested only in results. Seven out of eight applicants were rejected, and one out of every eight students failed to graduate.

This rigid selection of students before enrollment, of which every student was aware, aided in the maintenance of high standards throughout the program and cut academic casualties in the school to a minimum.

It has been said that the Navy school's program was successful because its administration viewed the problem confronting it squarely, determined exactly how much could be taught in the allotted time, determined exactly the nature, amount, and sequence of the subject matter that was to be taught, adopted those techniques for teaching specifically what was desired, drew up a plan of the course hour by hour, and exercised close control over the instructors who were to carry out the plan.

The original calculations and plans adopted in 1941 for Japanese, outlined above, still stand in the operation of the Navy course of Japanese, as well as Chinese (Foochow, Amoy, Mandarin, Cantonese), Malay, and Russian, which were added later. Some of the western European languages have been added to the offerings of the Navy language schools, all of which were transferred to Washington during 1946 to operate there as a permanent institution. In October 1946 instruction was being given in Japanese (14 months), Chinese (18 months), Russian (6 months), German (6 months), Portuguese (4 months), Italian (4 months), Spanish (3 months), and French (3 months).

The student-teacher ratio for the wartime programs (for Japanese, one to four or five; for Russian, one to three; and for Chinese, in some instances two teachers to one student) is almost unheard of in civilian educational centers. In contrast to the Army ASTP Foreign Area and Language Curriculum, which included an area study involving the geography, history, and the contemporary institutions of the country where the language is used, the Navy wartime language program made no provision for this feature. Cultural knowledge was acquired vicariously, for no attempt was made directly to teach Japanese or Chinese culture in the classroom.[3] The Navy expects to incorporate this feature, however.

[3] Cf. Axelrod, "The Navy Language School Program . . . Techniques," *op. cit.*

TEXTS AND AIDS FURNISHED BY THE NAVY
FOR ITS TRAINEES

Japanese

Creswell, H. T. *Dictionary of Military Terms* (English-Japanese, Japanese-English). University of Chicago Press.

Rose-Innes. *Beginners' Dictionary of Chinese-Japanese Characters & Compounds.* Harvard University Press.

Kenkyusha. *New Japanese-English Dictionary.* Harvard University Press.

Ueda. *Revised & Enlarged Edition, Dai Jiten.* Harvard University Press.

Fuzamba. *English-Japanese Dictionary.* Harvard University Press.

Ozaki. *Japanese-English Dictionary of Sea Terms.* University of California Press.

———. *Sosho Daijiten.*

Kenkyusha. *English-Japanese Dictionary.* University of California Press.

Naganuma. *Hyojun Nihongo Tokuhon,* Vols. I-VI. University of California Press.

———. *Teaching Aids,* Vols. I-VI. University of California Press.

Ashikaga. *List of 500 Kanji.* University of California Press.

———. *Lessons in Sosho.* University of California Press.

———. *Gyo-so Tokuhon.* University of California Press.

———. *Kaigun Tokuhon.* University of California Press.

Ishihara. *Rikagaku Jiten* [4] (Japanese Dictionary of Physics and Chemistry).

Gillis and Pai. *Japanese Surnames.*

———. *Japanese Personal Names.*

Chinese

Mathews, R. H. *Chinese-English Dictionary.* Harvard University Press.

———. *English Index to Mathews' Chinese-English Dictionary.* Harvard University Press.

Fenn, C. H., and Tseng, C. H. *Five Thousand Dictionary.* Harvard University Press.

Hua-Wen Ch'u Chieh. (Chinese Language Lessons). Stanford University Press.

Aldrich, H. S. *Practical Chinese* (Hua Yu Hsu Chih). Vols. I & II. Yale University Press.

Chih Pei Sha. *A Chinese First Reader.* University of California Press.

Japan Times. *Chinese-Manchurian Personal & Place Names.*

[4] Many such titles of foreign origin were privately printed for various government agencies and distributed to Navy language school trainees.

Malay

Sejarah Malayu, or *Malay Annals.*
Hikayat Abdullah—Bin Abdul Kadir, Munshi (Arabic Characters).
Hikayat Abdullah—Bin Abdul Kadir, Munshi (Roman Characters).
A Malay Dictionary (Malay-English, English-Malay).
Spat, C. *Maleische Taal.*
Winstedt, R. O. *Colloquial Malay* (A Simple Grammar with Conversations).
————. *An English-Malay Dictionary* (Roman Characters).
Wilkinson, R. J. *A Malay-English Dictionary* (Romanized).

Russian

Muller, V. K. *English-Russian Dictionary.* E. P. Dutton & Co.
————. *Russian-English Dictionary.* E. P. Dutton & Co.
O'Brien, M. A. *New Russian-English and English-Russian Dictionary.* Dover Publications, New York.
Bondar, D. *Bondar's Simplified Russian Method.* Pitman Publishing Corp., New York.
Patrick, George Z. *Elementary Russian Reader.* Pitman Publishing Corp., New York.
————. *Roots of the Russian Language.* Pitman Publishing Corp., New York.
————. *Advanced Russian Reader.* Pitman Publishing Corp., New York.
Patrick, George Z., and Noyes, G. R. *An Elementary Guide to Russian Pronunciation.* Pitman Publishing Corp., New York.

III. THE NAVY SCHOOLS OF MILITARY GOVERNMENT AND ADMINISTRATION

O N JUNE 17, 1942, the Navy Department decided to detail a number of naval officers to a program in military government and administration at Columbia University, where a curriculum was established emphasizing language and area studies similar to the ASTP and the CATS programs. Because of similar interests in military government, the Army and the Navy collaborated at many points in the establishment of their respective programs. As the school developed, there were parallel discussions in the War and Navy departments to establish the areas of primary responsibility for both the Army and the Navy.

It was generally understood that the Army would have jurisdiction in large land areas, such as Japan itself, and the Navy would have control in the islands of the Pacific. This difference in control with respect to military government explains the special program set up at Columbia for the Navy school. It is one problem to provide temporary military government for highly developed industrial regions, in Europe for example, where problems similar to our own are encountered. It is quite another problem to cope with the chaos of a newly conquered area in which the primitive peoples are utterly unlike those of western culture in their way of thinking and are faced with problems wholly alien to western civilization.

It was the task of the Navy's Military Government School to provide training for civil affairs officers to organize local government in the island areas of the Pacific which generally are not rich in resources and whose principal value would be as military and naval bases bulwarking the control of the Pacific. Civil affairs officers were to be attached to staffs of force commanders and remain in these island areas as integral parts of the naval command.

THE SCHOOL AT COLUMBIA UNIVERSITY

The school at Columbia was established after a series of conferences between Columbia University and the Navy Department, with the University taking the initiative and assuming the responsibility for the establishment of a program which would be acceptable to the Navy. The Navy school accepted almost without change the curriculum proposed by the Columbia faculty and entered into contractual agreements on execution of the accepted curriculum. This program was experimental in its early stages, but it did create a sound program which the Navy ultimately adopted as a permanent program of training for officer personnel who would be assigned to occupied areas both during the course of the war and in the postwar period.

The Navy was extremely liberal in allowing the faculty to have more or less its own way as to the subjects to be covered. As in the ASTP and the CATS, the heart of the Columbia curriculum was intensive study of the foreign language and a thorough inquiry into the characteristics of the place where the officer would go and of the people he would find when he reached there. The school was first established to continue for forty-eight weeks. Within a short period of time the course was cut to thirty-six weeks, and the whole curriculum had to be changed to meet the new time limit. The body and the basic concepts of the program, however, remained much the same. The shorter period of time meant primarily that there would be less intensive study in each area.

Program of study

The curriculum placed emphasis upon four categories of training: (1) language, (2) the study of native customs, (3) understanding of the governmental institutions—native and colonial—to which the populations of the Southwest Pacific and the Far East in general had been accustomed, and (4) certain technical aspects of military government itself.[1] This program is not unlike that of the Army, even to the detail of informing the trainees adequately as to the interpretation of history and the specific historic events and problems which are commonly accepted in the area itself. Unlike the Army program, which had

---

[1] Schuyler C. Wallace, "The Navy School of Military Government and Administration," *Annals of the American Academy of Political and Social Science*, CCXXXI (January 1944), 29–33.

an interest in military government on a broader scale and in which the trainees were assigned for study in a specific area, the Navy schools could not know in advance the exact area to which the officers were to be assigned. Consequently, the individual trainee had to learn all that he possibly could about several vast regions of divergent characteristics. Ideally, he had to emerge with a full knowledge of the land and people of the whole Pacific region, a thorough understanding of the psychology of each racial group in the region, a grasp of the economic organization and financial problems of all the widely different island groups, and a mastery of the techniques of conducting military government—not to mention the pertinent languages.

Since the Pacific Ocean areas are so vast and comprise such widely different island groups, several languages were required. In the actual development of the program, Colloquial Malay or Conversational Japanese and Melanesian Pidgin English were made required courses. In addition, officers who possessed any familiarity with other languages were encouraged to attend one of the refresher courses which were provided in Arabic, Chinese, Dutch, French, German, Italian, Japanese, Malay, Portuguese, Russian, and Spanish.

It was hoped that the officers upon graduation would be able to communicate in more than one language, thus facilitating the matter of their ultimate assignment. Here again the Navy, like the Army, was interested in the development of the oral skills, and the language programs were developed almost exclusively with this end in view.

We have outlined above the general interests of the Navy school, both with respect to the general areas involved and the types of general knowledge required. How was this program to be executed in the time limit determined for successful completion? The nine-month program was to be broken up into three successive terms. This meant giving basic instruction during the first term in the law and technique of military government, geography, anthropology, the history of earlier belligerent occupations, and basic language training. The second term was to concern a more intensive study of the areas involved, begin study in naval courts and boards, and undertake the study of elective or supplementary languages. For the third term, the officers' classroom work was to be reduced to a minimum and their time was to be devoted to what was called "laboratory work," involving projects requiring the development of military government plans for assigned areas. Along with these courses, there were numerous lectures in distinctly naval subjects, such as damage control, ship types, fleet organization, antisubmarine tactics, convoying methods, fire-fighting, and communications. In broad perspective, the program divided into its three-term components was somewhat as follows:

First term:

1. Seminar in military government problems
2. International law of military occupation
3. History of military occupations
4. Geography of possible areas of occupation
5. Anthropology of areas to be occupied
6. Miscellaneous lectures on military government
7. Language study

Second term:

1. Seminar projects in military government
2. History and government of areas to be occupied
3. Economics of military occupation
4. Anthropology
5. Lectures on naval subjects
6. Naval courts and boards
7. Language study

Third term:

1. Institutions and government of areas to be occupied
2. Seminar projects in military government
3. Language study

In addition, numerous special lectures and meetings were to be held on subjects related to this general program.

The specific curriculum for the first class at Columbia which lasted nearly ten months, as prepared by the instructional staff of the school follows:

PROGRAM OF TRAINING IN INTERNATIONAL ADMINISTRATION [2]

CURRICULUM: AUGUST 17–SEPTEMBER 28, 1942

International Administration 101A—3 points

A lecture series designed to introduce the students to problems of military occupation, economic rehabilitation, and relief, as these problems have been faced by the lecturers in the last several decades of the world's history.

International Administration 111A—3 points

An analysis of problems of military occupation, economic rehabilitation, and relief based upon the material provided in Administration 101A and extensive reading.

International Geography 101A—3 points

A survey of the physical and economic geography of the island areas of the Pacific and the lands adjacent thereto, with special studies of specific areas.

International Anthropology 101A—3 points

A general anthropological survey of the island areas of the Pacific and their people.

International Malay 101A—6 points

An introduction to conversational Malay based upon a vocabulary of from 300 to 500 words.

International Military Law 101A—1½ points

An analysis of the law of belligerent occupation with particular emphasis upon the relation of the military to the civilian populations.

CURRICULUM: SEPTEMBER 28–DECEMBER 19

International Administration 101B—3 points

A lecture series designed to introduce the students to problems of military occupation and administration, economic rehabilitation and relief, as these problems have been faced by the lecturers in the course of their several careers.

International Administration 111B—3 points

An analysis of problems of military occupation and administration, economic rehabilitation and relief, based upon the material provided in International Administration 101B and extensive reading.

[2] Office of the Chief of Naval Operations, "Military Government," Appendixes IX, X, XI, XII, and XIII (MS on file in Office of Naval History).

International Anthropology 101B—1½ points

A survey and analysis of certain island areas of the Pacific and their peoples.

International Anthropology 111B—3 points

An analysis of certain basic concepts of social science which bear directly upon the administration of native peoples.

International Military Law 101B—3 points

A study of the practice and procedure of provost courts and courts martial.

International Government 101B—3 points

An analysis of the governmental institutions and public policies of the Netherlands East Indies.

International Malay 101B—1 point

A continuation of the Malay previously given; designed further to increase facility in conversation.

Other languages as offered by the University

CURRICULUM: DECEMBER 28, 1942–MARCH 20, 1943

International Administration 101C—3 points

A lecture series designed to introduce the students to problems of military occupation and administration, economic rehabilitation and relief. Emphasis during this quarter will be upon economic problems.

International Administration 111C—3 points

A discussion of problems of military occupation and administration, economic rehabilitation and relief, based upon the material provided in International Administration 101C. In this connection an attempt will be made to formulate certain principles or generalizations applicable to the administration of occupied or liberated territories.

International Public Administration 101C—3 points

An analysis of organization and procedures in the conduct of the civil functions of government in occupied territory.

International Japanese Institutions 101C—3 points

An analysis of the institutions of Japan—social, economic, and political, which will contribute to a greater understanding of resources, motivation, and customary procedures of the enemy. Attention will be given to administrative practices in the mandated areas, the Asiatic mainland, and recently occupied territories.

International Colonial Institutions 101C—1½ points

An analysis of British Colonial practices in the island areas of the South Pacific.

International Relations of the Far East 101C—1½ points

An examination of political and social forces which have produced conflict in the Far East, with particular reference to their effect on the Occident and their relations to world politics; together with an analysis of the conditions prerequisite to a stable order.

International Pidgin English 101C—3 points

An introduction to Pidgin English.

Other languages as offered by the University

CURRICULUM: MARCH 22, 1943–JUNE 12, 1943

International Administration 101D—3 points

A lecture series designed to introduce the students to the problems of military government, economic rehabilitation and relief. Emphasis during this quarter will be divided between economic problems and problems of health.

International Organization 101D—1½ points

An analysis of those aspects of international organization, past and present, which are relevant to the work of military government and administration.

International Territorial Institutions 111D—1½ points

An analysis of the political institutions and public policies of the Philippines.

International Economics of War 101D—3 points

An analysis of the impact of the war upon the traditional economic institutions of the world.

International Colonial Institutions of Southeast Asia 101D—3 points

An analysis of the political institutions and public policies of Burma, Siam, Indo-China, and Malaya.

International Public Health 101D—1 point

A brief survey of public health conditions and policies in the island areas of the Pacific (May 17–May 29).

International Administration 111D—12 points

An intensive study of problems of military government in connection with certain selected areas.

General: The seminar as a whole will constitute a general staff or planning agency both for purposes of selecting the areas to be studied and also to hear reports from the regional committees.

Regional: After the appropriate areas have been selected, the seminar will be broken up into a series of regional committees which will engage in an extensive cooperative analysis of the problems inherent in the occupation of each specific area and the development of plans and procedures to be followed in the solution of these problems.

Note: In connection with certain aspects of these studies, e.g., legal and economic, health-specialists from the Schools of Law, Business, Agriculture, etc., will be brought in for consultation.

Other languages as offered by the University

It can be seen from the above curriculum that the Navy School of Military Government and Administration was primarily concerned in following a pattern of interdisciplinary studies quite similar to that established by the Army for its ASTP and CATS programs, with some degree of integration. An over-all provision was made for intensive study of the governing principles and optimum application of international law and public administration with a view to utilizing to a maximum practical degree the local institutions, procedures, and officials.

A general course in anthropology was to analyze for the trainees certain basic concepts of social science which bear directly on the administration of native peoples and to explain the great divergencies in culture between Far Eastern and Western civilizations. This basic and general survey of the whole area was to be followed by further courses which dealt with native institutions and customs of smaller and specific geographic areas.

The study of native customs and institutions was to be supplemented by a further series of courses to enable the trainees to understand the colonial institutions to which the native populations of the area under examination have been accustomed. A series of short courses in this connection dealing with the Netherlands East Indies, Burma, Indo-China, Malaya, and the smaller islands under British, French, and Portuguese control were established. The political institutions of Thailand and the Philippines, although not colonial in their character, were to receive similar attention.

To parallel these courses and the discussions and outside lectures that accompanied them, a series of seminars were to be organized for the third term, in which certain selected problems of military government would be presented for analysis. These problems were to be chosen in so far as possible to provide exercises in military government and to serve as techniques for integrating the program into a core of knowledge and for applying to military government the information acquired in the more formal courses of the program.

The seminars presented one of a series of courses during the first two semesters, but during the third term, the work of the seminars occupied one-half to two-thirds of the students' time. Some of these seminars which are devoted to assigned projects culminate in reports of 200 or 300 pages in length and are of a quality equal to that of the professional research organizations attached to the government.[3] These projects are really detailed studies of assigned areas, with plans for civil affairs organizations and recommendations as to civil affairs policies, quite similar to the problems that were provided for the CATS trainees. Such projects were devised for a large number of areas in the Pacific, including all those assigned to the Navy for military government as well as for a number of ports and port areas of Europe. This, in broad perspective, was the curriculum of the Navy School of Military Government and Administration at Columbia as it was originally conceived and as it developed.

Language study for the Navy school, like that of the Army, played an important role in the program. Since the program as a whole is centered on the Far Pacific region, the languages of that area were emphasized. All officers attending the school were required to take an intensive course either in Japanese or in Malay, the *lingua franca* of a vast area embracing perhaps 100,000,000 people. The officers likewise learn the rudiments of Melanesian Pidgin, that odd but useful jargon, 85 percent English, which is spoken in varying styles from the Solomons and Bismarcks across to New Guinea. Malay and Melanesian Pidgin are "trade languages" of special value to naval personnel since they are most current in the ports of the southwest Pacific.

[3] Wallace, *op. cit.*

Some officers had a working knowledge of Japanese or Chinese before entering the naval service and simply had to take refresher courses in them. Others had to start colloquial Japanese from the beginning. Others took Dutch, Arabic, French, Spanish, Italian, German, or any other language which might be of use in either the European or the Asiatic theaters. Most of the language instruction was built around the intensive methods adopted by the Army, with emphasis on conversation rather than on grammatical structure. The vocabulary was practical and centered about the war and governmental functions.

Teaching emphasis was placed on the spoken language rather than on the rules of grammar and literary style. In addition to the regular instructors, extensive use was made of natives or other persons fluent in the language being studied, called "informants." These informants, like the drill-masters in the Army language classes, were to provide conversational practice for the students. Each language group worked under several instructors and informants for the purpose of acquiring greater conversational facility and a corresponding improvement in ability to comprehend. During the nine-month course, the student officers received 480 hours of language instruction.[4]

The changes in the curriculum during the existence of the school reflect changes of over-all planning brought about by the progress of the war. The earlier groups of students undertook studies concerning the Dutch East Indies and the islands of the South and Southeast Pacific. Gradually, the later sections took up area studies of territories which had been under Japanese control before the outbreak of war. The study of Malay, Dutch, and Pidgin English was dropped altogether, and the Chinese or Japanese languages were studied by all the students of the later sections.

Personnel and their selection

The naval program of training for military government was conceived in the most modest of terms for the reason that offen-

---

[4] Office of the Chief of Naval Operations, "Military Government" (MS on file in Office of Naval History), I, 10.

sive action by U.S. forces in the Pacific was then in the seemingly remote future.[5] Standards for selection set by the Bureau of Naval Personnel were high. Applications were invited from civilians between the ages of twenty-eight and forty-five with broad professional training, ability, and experience in one or more of a number of business and professional fields. Residence abroad and linguistic proficiency were desirable, but not required, from the beginning. One means of lightening the burden of training and of shortening the period of attendance was through the choice, wherever possible, of officers or civilians who already possessed special knowledge of Pacific and Far Eastern areas, because of residence there or previous professional or commercial experience. Applications from such persons were forwarded by the field officer of the procurement branch to the Bureau of Naval Personnel where an informal selection board of five senior officers selected a group of 29 students which constituted the first class at Columbia. A similar procedure was followed in the selection of the three subsequent classes, with more emphasis on successful administrative experience. Beginning with the fifth class, around December 1, 1943, appointments were made almost entirely from among qualified officer applicants who were available for transfer from other branches of the service. In choosing line officers for the later classes at Columbia, a more rigid classification of personnel needs by functional qualification was employed so that a wider scale of job needs would be satisfied thereby.

Classes were admitted into the Columbia establishment regularly at three-month intervals, varying in size from twenty-five to sixty officers. This group consisted of officers from the Regular Navy, the Naval Reserve, the Marine Corps, the Army, the Coast Guard, and the Public Health Service. There was, throughout the existence of these programs, in both the Army and the Navy, a more or less constant interchange of personnel from the two main arms of the services in their respective schools. In the beginning and for the first two sections, there was an equal number of civilians who followed the curriculum. How-

[5] *Ibid.*, p. 24.

ever, for security reasons, it was necessary to separate the civilians from the officer personnel. Both groups continued with the third session in separate programs of study.

The following table shows the number of trainees who entered and those who were graduated:[6]

Section	Reported	Graduated
First	29	26
Second	26	22
Third	39	33
Fourth	66	64
Fifth	39	30
Sixth	56	49
Seventh	57	51
Eighth	80	72
Total	392	347

The 347 who were graduated may be regarded as having completed the course, although in the later sections a number were withdrawn shortly before completion of the scheduled course because of the urgent need elsewhere of officers trained in military government. Sixty-six students, having completed the requirements for a higher degree than that held by other student officers, received the degree of master of arts which the University conferred upon them.

The original plan called for training of 500 officers. The school was unable to train this number, due to lack of procurement.

THE SCHOOL AT PRINCETON UNIVERSITY

The accelerated tempo of the war in the Pacific brought about quite suddenly an urgent need for an even larger number of military government officers than the 500 originally contemplated. This caused the Navy to begin plans for the establishment of another school at Princeton University to train in a shorter period of time more officers than could be trained at Columbia.

[6] *Ibid.*, p. 11.

In spite of the changes in the curriculum, the shortening of the period of attendance, and the withdrawing of students before completion of the courses, the school was successful in meeting the serious responsibilities placed upon it.

On October 3, 1944, the first class of 447 officers began the much shorter program which had been set up at Princeton. This new program was the outgrowth of the earlier classes at Columbia, and since many more men had to be trained, larger classes were required and a shorter period of attendance was established. It was to be twelve weeks as against the earlier program which lasted nine months. There were but three classes to enter this school before it was decommissioned and the school set up elsewhere on a postwar basis.

According to a memorandum[7] dated June 27, 1944, the program was to present in as detailed and complete a form as was possible in the twelve-week period, a knowledge of the history, geography, economics, and customs of the peoples of various areas of the Pacific. The course was to be fifty hours in length broken down as follows: Japan, twenty hours; China, ten hours; the Pacific, five hours; Southeast Asia, five hours; area study, covering in detail the area of most immediate interest, ten hours.

Language study, for this briefer curriculum was limited to thirty-five hours. It was designed to give each officer a vocabulary and use of about two hundred carefully selected nontechnical words in the language of greatest immediate interest. No formal grammar was to be taught. Such grammar as the trainees acquired was to be embodied in sentence patterns and phrases commonly used. This extremely rudimentary beginning was designed to serve as a basis for further language learning in the islands.

This program, however, did not evolve for the school at Princeton. It should be added for the record that in the permanently established school now located on the Pacific coast, language study is a required course in the curriculum. The final program, quoted below, actually contained no language study at all.

[7] Office of the Chief of Naval Operations, "Military Government," Princeton Section, Vol. I, Appendix I. Courses 6 and 7 only cited here.

SUMMARY OF TRAINING OF THE NAVY SCHOOL OF MILITARY
GOVERNMENT AT PRINCETON UNIVERSITY [8]

1. *The Practice of Civil Affairs*
   Background course dealing with past experience in civil affairs. Emphasis is upon different types of occupation and specific problems related to varying methods of civil affairs organization.

2. *Seminar on General Functions of a Civil Affairs Officer*
   The integration of readings and lectures on military government. Application of this knowledge to specific problems. Direction of the seminar will be rotated among student officers. Each student is required to prepare a term paper.

3. *International Law of Military Government*
   Essential backgrounds in international law.

4. *Labor*
   International law, economics, and welfare in relation to labor problems.

5. *Police Functions in Military Government*
   Relationship of the civil affairs officer to police action.

6. *Military Courts*
   Lectures on the operation of military courts in a belligerent occupation and practice, or moot, courts. Moot courts include demonstrations of trials conducted through interpreters.

7. *Economics and Finance*
   Principles and examples of occupational economics; currencies, wages, inflation, and black markets.

8. *Peoples and Customs*
   A study of the physical geography of Far Eastern areas. The history, physical and human geography, sociology, economics, and culture of Japan, the China coast, Taiwan, and certain Japanese islands.

9. *Military Organization and Procedure*
   Other branches, arms and services in joint and combined operations. Specialized naval functions.

10. *Tropical Sanitation*
    General problems of public health, and methods of disease control.

11. *Public Health and Hygiene*
    General problems of sanitation.

[8] *Curriculum, Navy School of Military Government,* prepared by the educational staff of the school and Standards and Curriculum Division, Training, Bureau of Naval Personnel, September 1944.

12. *Engineering in Civil Affairs*
Elements of engineering of value to the civil affairs officer in the field. Map reading and elementary map sketching.

13. *Welfare*
Problems of feeding, housing, clothing, transporting, and registering of displaced persons, prisoners, released prisoners, internees, and enemy nationals.

Whereas the control of the program was under a faculty of civilian instructors at Columbia, the situation was completely reversed at Princeton. Control of the program was under military and naval officers. To the group of instructors which came from the Columbia school, there were added officers from the various theaters of operation who were primarily responsible, because of their war experiences, for maintaining an up-to-the-minute, stimulating, and practical program based on actual field operations. Since there were both Army and Navy men in the classes, the Army supplied instructors from its own ranks. Supervision of instructors was on a departmental basis.

Study outlines for the presentation of material were of two types: the *subject-matter* type of outline, which attempted to carry complete detail and which, in fact, served as a text; and the *table of contents* type, which merely served as a guide to the organization of the lecture. These types of outlines had value in assisting the instructor to present his material briefly and stripped of all unnecessary references. Cold facts were presented unadorned by any lucubrations. They had value also in enabling the student to concentrate on the lecture and to be spared the necessity of rapidly jotting down notes, some of which would inevitably be inaccurate and incomplete.

For this program, various forms of aids were used, such as map studies, regional analyses of numerous coastal cities in Asia—including all pertinent geographical controls such as streets, highways, bridges, coast lines, airports, parks, or any similar recognizable area—motion pictures, outside lectures, moot courts, and seminars. Special procedures were outlined for the utilization of training films. Every instructor was obliged to preview the motion pictures or the filmstrips which were prescribed in the curriculum to become thoroughly familiar with the contents. The instructor was to assure himself beforehand that he had all needed equipment in the classroom and that satisfactory physical conditions prevailed. Before showing the films, he was to tell his men what film they were to see and what principal points they were expected to learn from it. After the film had been shown, the instructor had to summarize again the principal points involved. He had to encourage class discussion and make every effort to ascertain by written or oral questions whether the special points of the film had been learned by the class. Wherever possible, the material taught by the film was to be put into practice immediately on actual equipment.

OUTCOMES OF THE ENTERPRISE

The total number of personnel trained in the Navy schools of military government was 1,412. In addition, 201 line officers were assigned to military government duties without training.

The experience of the military government schools at Columbia and Princeton serves to corroborate the claims which were made for the Army language classes, namely, that it is possible to teach languages in such a way that students can communicate in a short period of time—three, six, or nine months, depending on the language. It also proved that training in government and administration is not the exclusive prerogative of any one discipline, but is instead a grouping of disciplines cutting across both departmental and faculty lines.[9] It showed further that, by attempting to integrate the knowledge required about a specific area by focusing several disciplines on that area, a more truly complete picture of that area would result.

[9] Wallace, *op. cit.*

IV. THE JAPANESE LANGUAGE
SCHOOLS OF THE ARMY

THE MISSION OF the Military Intelligence Service Language
School [1] was to train personnel in Japanese as translators,
interpreters, and interrogators for the field forces. The personnel assigned to this school were primarily Nisei, or Americans
of Japanese ancestry although there were a few Caucasians.
The initial school was set up at the Presidio of San Francisco on
November 1, 1941, as the Fourth Army Intelligence School, to
give refresher training in basic Japanese and to provide sufficient
training in military Japanese, organization of the Japanese Army,
interrogation, and similar subjects to qualify a few highly selected
Nisei for the tasks to which they would later be assigned. Four
instructors and sixty students comprised this early school.

The school was moved, however, to Camp Savage, Minnesota,
shortly after the outbreak of war between the United States and
Japan, and on May 25, 1942, the school came under the direct
supervision of the War Department. Its mission was the same
as that of the earlier school established at the Presidio. A secondary mission called for the training of a few Caucasian officers
and enlisted men to serve as language officers to work with the
Nisei in the field. Though the Caucasian personnel had a primary responsibility of insuring loyalty on the part of the Nisei,
they were also necessary to insure that what translations were
made would be rendered into idiomatic English.

It developed, later, that the MISLS was too advanced for
Caucasians unless they had had considerable previous training or
experience in the language. For this reason, in November 1942,
the War Department decided to establish a one-year course in
Japanese at the University of Michigan. The first class began
January 5, 1943, with 21 instructors and about 150 trainees in
the newly established school which came to be known as the Army

---

[1] Cf. "The Training History of the Military Intelligence Service Language School"
(MSS on file in Historical Division, War Department Special Staff). See Bibliography.

Japanese Language School.² Seven classes totaling 780 trainees in all were graduated from this school. As the instruction at the MISLS was of an advanced nature, and the trainees were primarily Nisei and thus were learning their own language, the MISLS has only incidental interest for the future language programs of civilian education. On the other hand, the school established at the University of Michigan, since it concerned primarily Caucasians and therefore relates to the learning of a second language, may have some import for civilian education, especially in the teaching of Japanese.

The objective of the school was to give basic training in spoken and written Japanese and to present as much factual knowledge as possible about Japan and the Japanese people, so that with advanced training at the MISLS the trainees would be fitted for combat intelligence and for military government work in Japan or any area where the language is essential.

In accordance with the terms of the contract, each class was to have forty-nine weeks of instruction, twenty-four hours each week. Furloughs of one week were first scheduled at the end of a sixteen- or seventeen-week period, and later at the end of a twelve- or thirteen-week period. Classes for instruction in the language normally had seven or eight students, grouped according to their proficiency in the language. Such classes were thought to be large enough for competition and yet small enough for individual attention. The twenty-four hours of instruction were broken down as follows: ten hours on the spoken language; two hours of viewing Japanese movies; five hours of reading; five hours of studying and using characters, or *kanji;* and two hours of examinations. In addition, students who were poor or not up to the week's standard (usually a B average) were obliged to attend the daily supervised study periods during the following week. This twenty-four-hour program was scheduled into four hours of classes Monday through Friday, with a two-hour session viewing Japanese films late Monday afternoon and two hours of

² Source material is found in "The Army Japanese Language School," Annex No. 3 in "The Training History of the Military Intelligence Service Language School" (MS on file in Historical Division, War Department Special Staff); and "Japanese Language Programs, University of Michigan, World War II" (MS on file in Historical Division, War Department Special Staff), Vol. I, Chapter II.

examinations usually on Saturday morning. Since there was a spoken-language hour and a reading hour in the morning, a *kakitori,* or dictation hour, and a spoken-language hour in the afternoon, the day began and ended with drill in the spoken language.

The students comprised, according to the records, one of the best selected units in the Army. They had high IQ's and high ratings in the Army General Classification Test. Some of them were BIJ's; that is, they had either been "born in Japan" or they had "been in Japan." In the later classes, a high percentage of the students came with extensive previous training amounting to as much as one year in various ASTP units. Because of the high grade of trainees and the motivation provided by the war, discipline was excellent. No student was dismissed from the school without a complete investigation of the facts by the school director. Usually he was given a stiff warning and a chance to remain if he improved.

The instructors were native speakers of the language belonging to one of three more or less distinct groups: Issei, Kibei, or Nisei. The Issei are persons of Japanese ancestry who were born in Japan and who have come to the United States as immigrants. The Kibei are sons and daughters of Issei who were born in the United States and who went to Japan for a major part of their education. The Nisei are also children of Issei who have spent most of their lives in the United States and were educated here. The Issei and Kibei are more definitely native speakers of Japanese, while the Nisei are more able to understand the thought processes of those whose mother tongue is English. Consequently, both groups had their parts to play in the program.

THE ORAL LANGUAGE

The oral-aural approach is used exclusively during the first five or six weeks. No reference is made to grammar. In the early stages, the students mimic the instructor's pronunciation in unison. The materials used in the beginning are conversational scripts or short dialogues involving greetings, questions, and phrases which occur in everyday life, such as directions for conducting the classroom work, greetings in the street and elsewhere, phrases related to the home, making visits, shopping, or going to the doctor or the dentist, all in the form of pattern sentences. Each phrase is learned by rote after numerous repetitions. This mimicry and memorization the school designates as the first stage of learning the spoken language which attempts to fix pronunciation habits. The second stage concerns the development of these pattern sentences learned in the first stage into the endless variety that may exist for the beginner by mere change of a word. "How much is the fare?" becomes "How much is the cake?", for example, with an endless possibility of variations. There are certain locally prepared "speech patterns" involving a whole series of sentences which successively illustrate the same grammatical point. These lead from the more simple to the more complex. Pronunciation is corrected as the work progresses with an attempt to adhere to the standard pronunciation of Tokyo, that is, the pronunciation of persons who belong to the middle-class or higher. The third stage in the development of the spoken language concerns the development of oral fluency.

About the third month of the program, a series of "speech hours" is arranged in which new materials are introduced, no longer using isolated sentences, but connected discourse. Since it is assumed that by now some grammar has been learned, however rudimentary, the study of grammar enters the picture in various ways, but always related to the spoken form of the language. An attempt is made to concentrate on the development of ready and easy flow of speech, and to this end a series of topics based on the individual pattern sentences already learned are assigned to students to develop. These usually relate to places, things, or situations which will confront the trainee later on, such as: Tokyo as I know it, the things I want to see in Tokyo, the largest city I know, the city I like best in America, the chief products of my birthplace, Japanese fairy tales, great men and their boyhood, and so on.

When some degree of facility in speaking the language has been achieved in this fashion, the students continue on to its more technical uses until emphasis is gradually centered about military and administrative situations.

Compositions are assigned once a week on the reading material covered. These papers embody language-content, grammar, vocabulary, ready-learned phrases which the students already know, and usually are couched in a conversational rather than literary style. These can be used as guides in speaking. They are corrected and returned on the following day with the major corrections clarified by the teacher. The corrected compositions are rewritten and returned with the originals for filing, thus providing a written record from week to week of each student's progress. If the students write as they speak, then one has again an excellent opportunity of seeing how well they control the language they are learning.

Attempts were made to conduct the "speech hours" based on vocabulary lists. These attempts were not too successful, due to lack of properly prepared lists. Doi's *Basic Japanese-English List* was used. Because of the lack of verbs and descriptive words to accompany the nouns contained in the list, a new one entitled *A Basic English-Japanese Word List Arranged According to Topics* was prepared by the staff to correct this deficiency. A member of the staff prepared a series of pictures illustrating the words in this basic list, and the two came to be used as a basis for some of the speech hours. Further lists prepared by the staff for the oral work of the speech hours will be found at the end of this section.

Japanese films, lantern slides, and speech contests all aided in the further learning of the spoken language. The school has tried in its oral program to give its students a broad basic vocabulary. The words found in the elementary texts pertain to such matters as the body, dress, dwelling, food, and drink. Various cultural aspects of Japanese life are taken up, followed by specialization in the fields of geography, the military establishment, and civil administration. In teaching this vocabulary, it is also necessary to teach grammar and, at the same time, to prepare the student to attain the greatest possible flexibility in the use of grammatical forms. Though errors in pronunciation, grammar, or word usage should never be condoned, the drive toward fluency sometimes has meant that accuracy takes a secondary place.

READING

The basic readers are the Naganuma readers, Books I, II, and III, already mentioned in an earlier section. While these readers contain a more or less conversational type of material, they are written in characters rather than romanized script. Naturally the effort required for reading characters is much greater than that required when romanized script is used. It is the eyes rather than the ears that first receive an outside stimulus. When characters are used, beginning students have no clues as to how the characters should be pronounced. Reading, however, does not begin until the fifth or sixth week, which means that students have already had nearly 150 hours of the language. To make the transfer from the purely oral work to the reading and written work, especially with characters instead of the romanized script, the reading lessons are divided into six successive parts or stages.

First, there is a review of the previous day's lesson usually done by a student who gives a rapid, well-modulated reading. A few questions are asked regarding the meaning of certain passages to assure general comprehension. This is followed by the reading of the new lesson by the instructor at a normal pace, or the phrases are read one by one with the students repeating in unison. For comprehension purposes, renditions into simpler or a different Japanese are made, and sometimes various passages and vocabulary items are dictated to see whether the student can actually reproduce the characters, which is a step beyond mere comprehension. The third part includes a brief period of questions and answers in Japanese based on the new lesson. Next the students are required to read the passage, six or seven sentences at a stretch. Corrections are made as the students read. A second and a third reading by the same student of the same passage may be necessary to assure that the passage has been mastered.

The chief object of the reading lesson is to see that the students respond easily to written characters, study and learn them in sequence, comprehend their meaning, and transform what is seen and understood into fluent, well-modulated, and meaningful speech. The fifth part involves an attempt to find out how much the students have learned from the reading passage. Where the Naganuma readers are used, this is done by the use of the accompanying workbooks which require the fill-in type of response. There are also questions and answers on a student-student basis as well as a teacher-student basis. If the reading passage contains dialogue, the teacher may ask the students to act out the passage, or the students may be asked to give a summary of the entire lesson. The sixth and last stage is a preview of the next lesson, with the entire passage read for the students' benefit.

Translation, which was once a formal part of the program involving a full half-hour period each reading lesson, was discarded from the program primarily because the teachers, for the most part Nisei, were not sufficiently versed in English to check on accuracy of translation and also because the use of English in this part of the program tended to create a need for it even in the spoken-language classes.

One of the virtues of the Naganuma readers is the introduction of 1,100 frequently used characters on a gradated scale and the predominant use of words that are native in origin throughout Book I.

WRITING

The students are required to learn in the Naganuma readers two sets of *kana,* or phonetic characters, and 1,100 of the *kanji,* or Chinese characters, borrowed by the Japanese for their written language. The *kana* include the 48 angular forms known as the *katakana* and the corresponding cursive forms known as the *hiragana.* The two sets of *kana* are learned in the first two weeks as explained in the school director's *Introduction to Japanese Writing* and in the first part of Naganuma's Book I. The *kana* are dictated either singly or in word groups, the students performing either at their seats or at the blackboard. The 1,100 *kanji* are taught so that the students can recognize them, read them, know their meanings, and write them either in free compositions or in controlled passages such as a dictation. Usually the pace is slow and but five or six characters are learned per day. These are introduced to the students as they appear in the Naganuma readers. The *kanji* are for the most part introduced to the students prior to their actual use in a written script and are therefore learned in advance of, and quite apart from, the reading text. Dictations are corrected the day they are given and returned on the same day or, at the latest, the first hour of the next day.

EXPECTED PROFICIENCY AT THE END OF THE YEAR

Students who have had no previous training in Japanese are able to ask for food, shelter, clothing, and transportation, and to ask and understand the responses to pointed questions of considerable idea content. It is believed that the trainees are able to interrogate prisoners of war and to gather information of considerable tactical value. In reading, the content of the first three books of the Naganuma readers was easily finished in the time limit. However, to assure ability to read with ease newspapers, magazines, reference works, military orders, or any material which educated adult Japanese would read, the advanced training at Camp Savage (later Fort Snelling) was necessary. The students must know the 1,100 *kanji* or Chinese characters of the Naganuma Books I, II, and III, and in addition, the two sets of 48 *kana* or phonetic characters. Some students acquire as many as 1,600 characters and a familiarity with grammar forms that are peculiar to the literary style so that they can handle adult material with some degree of competence.

This initial course of one year was considered sufficient for the students to enter the more advanced school, the Military Intelligence Service Language School, located at Fort Snelling, Minnesota. Here they acquire a larger vocabulary and learn more of the *kanji* characters (up to as many as 2,100) in preparation for the more specialized courses of the advanced program.

INSTRUCTIONAL MATERIALS

Special texts or other materials prepared or used by the staff are listed on the next page:

For the Spoken Language

To fix proper pronunciation habits and to give beginning students a fund of common expressions:

Introduction to Spoken Japanese
Japanese Pronunciation Drill
Modern Conversational Japanese, by Yamagiwa

To give the students a knowledge of the basic sentence patterns into which new vocabulary items, successively learned, can be easily fitted:

Japanese Speech Patterns, Books I, II, III, IV, V
Conversations in Japanese

To increase vocabulary, both general and technical, so that the trainees will be equipped not only to handle everyday situations, but to make themselves effective in military and administrative situations:

Informal Conversations in Japanese, including Plays and Movie Synopses
The Geography of Japan
Military Conversations in Japanese
Conversations in Japanese for Military Government Officers
A Set of Six Japanese Topographical Sheets
Condensed Time-Tables of Japanese Railways
An English-Japanese Vocabulary of Words Arranged According to Subjects
A Place-Name List for the Japanese Empire
A Vocabulary for Architecture: English-Japanese
An English-Japanese Glossary of Industrial Terms
Vocabulary on Communications: English-Japanese
A Glossary of Censorship and Communication Terms in Japanese
Terms Relating to the Appreciation of Motion Pictures
An English-Japanese Glossary for Civil Affairs Officers

For the Written Language

For the basic facts pertaining to the Japanese system of writing:

Introduction to Japanese Writing, by Yamagiwa

For the stroke-order of the Chinese characters or *kanji* and general information pertaining to them:

Charts for the Writing of Chinese Characters
Kanji Book for 1,100 Characters in the Naganuma *Tokuhon,* Books I, II, III
A Book of *on* Pronunciations for the 100 Characters in the Naganuma Readers, Books I, II, III

List of 500 *Kanji* which appear in Book I, Naganuma Readers, by
E. Ashikaga

Chinese-Japanese Character Cards, Series I, by N. Naganuma

For reading ability and transfer from materials that use primarily the
grammar forms of the spoken language to materials containing distinctly literary grammatical forms:

Naganuma Readers, Books I, II, III, IV, together with the vocabulary
lists and the concordances prepared for them

Modern Conversational Japanese

The Modern Japanese Written Language

Jinjo Shogaku Chirisho (Elementary School Geography), selections

Jinjo Shogaku Rekishi (Elementary School History), selections

Heigo Tokuhon (Military Reader), Book I, with vocabulary and
concordance

General References and Aids

Kankyusha's New Japanese-English Dictionary, by Takenobu. Harvard University Press, 1942

An English-Japanese Dictionary of the Spoken Language, by Satow-
Ishibashi. American Ed., South Pasadena, P. D. and Ione Perkins,
1943

Beginners' Dictionary of Chinese-Japanese Characters, by Rose-Innes.
Harvard University Press, 1942

Daijiten, by M. Ueda, etc. Harvard University Press, 1942

Most of the above listed materials are in print, lithoprint, or multi-
lith. Except for the last four items listed as references and aids, most
of the other material listed was either prepared or reproduced at the
University of Michigan, Ann Arbor.

Training Aids

Movies, usually 3 showings were presented.

Recording Machines: In the early stages nearly all of the material to
be learned is recorded. Three or four sets are made and these are
loaned to students like books for study purposes.

Lantern-Slide Lectures: Used for showing pictures of the country
under study, but also for flashing Chinese characters which students
are asked to pronounce on sight.

Mirrophone: Usually both instructor and student voices are recorded
at the same time, with instructor asking the student to mimic him, or
with the instructor correcting the student's pronunciation.

V. FOREIGN AREA AND LANGUAGE PROGRAM OF THE ASTP

THE FOREIGN AREA and Language Program of the Army is similar to the Navy language program, but varies in degree of intensiveness. In the Navy school, the trainee's entire time was devoted to the study of the language. While the Army wanted competent speakers of the language, it also desired that its trainees acquire a knowledge of the contemporary history, institutions, and geography of the area in which the language is used. Consequently, the trainees in the ASTP program did not devote all their time to language study; part of the program called for specific knowledge of the area, in the ratio of about three-fifths of the student's time for language and approximately two-fifths of his time for area study. In the early stages, however, area study received the greater emphasis.

A further distinctive feature of the ASTP program was its emphasis on the spoken form of the language and its comprehension, while the Navy school sought to develop the skills of reading and writing at the same time as the oral skills. The time element for the Navy school was determined to be, for some languages at least, much longer than that for the Army. The ASTP language programs were established to require the same time for completion in all languages—about nine months.[1] The area study which was to accompany the study of the language was to complement it, so that in a sense one would aid the other in the furtherance of the main objective. In some instances area study was conducted in the foreign tongue,[2] especially when there were qualified personnel to perform this function. However, in a great many instances, this part of the program was conducted in English. For beginners, the English language was a necessity.

---

[1] Originally the time available for training was two terms of twelve weeks each. As it later became apparent that the desired fluency could not be achieved in that time, a third term was added. "History of the ASTP" (MS on file in Historical Division, War Department Special Staff), p. 123.

[2] One of the aims of the Intensive Language Program was to acquaint the student first with a speaking knowledge of the language and to develop in him the ability to comprehend, so that, after a brief period of study, the student would be able to use the language in the classroom.

There are three separate agencies which gave this program, at least for the Army: the School of Military Government at Charlottesville, the Civilian Affairs Training Schools, and the Army Specialized Training Program. The Navy School of Military Government and Administration at Columbia, later transferred to Princeton, is also related to these programs. While there was close cooperation between the Army and Navy, the Navy school had certain fundamental characteristics of its own and for that reason has been treated as a separate unit in this report.

A brief word is necessary to explain the origin of these programs and the curricula which were provided to meet them. Early in the spring of 1942, the Provost Marshal General was charged with the responsibility of training a few hundred Army officers for military government duty in occupied territory.[3] Where was he to turn for a suitable curriculum for this purpose? In the archives of the War Department someone had found the lone manuscript copy of the report made by an officer who had had experience with the military government program in Germany after the last war.[4] This report convinced the military and civil officials that special training for officers who were assigned to military government duty would be required if there was to be an improvement over conditions prevailing in the last war. These conditions revealed not only lack of training—for there was no training—but also considerable misunderstanding of the problems confronting such an officer, as well as total inability to cope with the language or to understand the people and their environment. Consequently, the School of Military Government was established at Charlottesville to train these officers.[5]   A little later the Military Government Division was created in the office of the Provost Marshal General to recruit officers and assign them to training.[6]

One of the earliest determinations of this division was that Army officers assigned to Civil Affairs would have to be supported

[3] "History of Training, Military Government" (MS on file in Historical Division, War Department Special Staff), p. 4.
[4] Ibid., p. 3.
[5] Approval granted by War Department Letter, AG 352 (3-4-42) MT-C.
[6] "History of Training, Military Government," op. cit., p. 8.

by small forces of military police under the command of commissioned and noncommissioned officers trained for the special problems of occupied territory.[7] This training was the special task of the Military Government Divison.[8] The personnel for this program breaks down into two groups: those trained by the ASTP for whom the Foreign Area and Language Program was prepared and those trained in the Civil Affairs Training Schools, for whom a similar program of shorter duration was provided. The officers trained in the Civil Affairs Training Schools and the School of Military Government at Charlottesville were to direct the activities of the occupational military police who were trained in the ASTP. These officers went first to an Army post for instruction in theory and practice of military government and then to the CATS for area and language study and application of military government principles to the situations which would be encountered in the occupied country.[9]

Language study was not a primary objective of the School of Military Government at Charlottesville and was offered only intermittently.[10] The course was of short duration, usually eight weeks. Since what language there was did not involve any new or distinctive features, the school at Charlottesville has only incidental value to this study in that language was considered a part of military government training. On the other hand, in the ASTP and the CATS, language and area study present such a different aspect from that which prevails in the traditional civilian program that it is of special significance for civilian education. The school at Charlottesville, which did not have a distinctive language program of its own, however, played an important role. Out of its military government curriculum came the idea of an integrated language and area program.

The Military Government Division was established at about the same time that the program for the ASTP was being prepared, the first sessions of which were scheduled for opening in

[7] Charles S. Hyneman, "The Wartime Area and Language Courses," *Bulletin of the American Association of University Professors, XXXI* (Autumn 1945), 434-47.
[8] "History of Training, Military Government," *op. cit.,* p. 4. (Memorandum, 10 January 1942.)
[9] *Ibid.,* p. 38.
[10] *Ibid.,* p. 44.

April 1943. This fact is significant, for, if the Chief of the Military Government Division had not envisaged the entire Foreign Area and Language Program for his own future trainees, and had not gone to the Chief of the ASTD to acquaint him with the program and urged him to accept and approve it, there might not have been an area and language curriculum as we now know it. Of course, the Military Government Division could have set up its own program at Charlottesville and elsewhere. Yet it is doubtful that such a program would have been successful because, at the military government schools, so much emphasis was always placed on other problems concerning military tactics, law, and administration that nonmilitary matters were nearly always relegated to a secondary place or crowded out altogether.

There are numerous reasons for the establishment of a sound training program for military government in occupied territory, especially if those undertaking this function have in mind the international law governing this activity. According to international law, it is the duty of the military commander, who is ex officio the military governor of the occupied area, to preserve, as far as military necessity will permit, the established institutions and customs of the area. Military government is, in a certain sense, superstructure erected over the local setup. The ideal military government will be one which can integrate the local laws, customs, institutions, and economy of an occupied area and this superimposed military control with a minimum of disturbance to the former and a maximum of control by the latter.

It becomes readily apparent that, in the days of modern warfare with the airplane and its destructive power, military government is carried out under the most difficult and chaotic conditions. When the enemy has been defeated and his country occupied, the establishment of peace and order is the first consideration. When homes have been destroyed, public services have been damaged and wrecked nearly beyond repair, and food supplies have run low, means must be found to restore them. In short, when the entire economy of the country has been destroyed and a state of chaos prevails, disease, famine, and pestilence may not be far away. After local officials have either fled or have become no longer able to function in such areas, in the name of humanity and reason as well as in the name of international law, the populace, civilians—men, women, and children—cannot be permitted to perish in the general confusion which prevails. For this general confusion some kind of order must be established.

On the other hand, because the nation has been defeated, these very civilians, unfriendly toward the occupying forces, may constitute a great peril to the military commander. They may attempt to disrupt his installations or to meddle with his lines of communication, and they may be in contact with an enemy not yet completely subdued. The military commander must preserve the military situation and insure a continuance of his military success. At the same time he must use all means in his power to give assistance, consistent with military necessity, to these unfortunate civilians who have been caught in the meshes of combat. Consequently, he needs all kinds of qualified assistants to help him in the discharge of his duties—lawyers, engineers in all fields of public works and utilities, experts in public safety, health, communications, money and banking, currency and exchange, and price control. Not only must personnel in these various skills be available, but they must be acquainted with the general principles operating in the intricate field of military government. At the same time, they must know in considerable detail about the country in which they are to operate. They must know something about the habits, the customs, the thinking and the reactions, and above all, the language of the people upon whom this military control is imposed.[11]

In the face of these problems which were certain to be met in the prosecution of the war, a suitable program had to be arranged to train officers and enlisted men to handle them. It was to fulfill this need that the Foreign Area and Language Program was created, first in the ASTP, and then modified slightly to serve a shorter period of training in the CATS. Since the problems of police administration have no particular interest or significance for peacetime education, they will be omitted here. The special curriculum for this project will be found in Appendix B.

Some of the earlier details concerning the broad aspects of the

[11] For a general description of reasons for military government, see War Department Field Manual FM 27-5, particularly paragraph 11.

curriculum were that the course should be planned for nine months, that most of the men would be trained for service in Japan or Germany, and that at least a small number of men should be trained for any place where an American army might conceivably take and hold territory.

GENERAL OBJECTIVES AND CONTENT

As a preliminary step to the establishment of the Foreign Area and Language Program, a conference was held at Charlottesville, April 16–18, 1943, to determine the subject matter of instruction in detail. The discussion at Charlottesville was to be guided by the following general statement:[12]

The curriculum will consist of three parts or subdivisions described as follows:

1. *Special Knowledge of Characteristics and Conditions of Areas of Occupation*

This will consist of (*a*) lectures, supervised project work and discussion relating to the people, their physical environment, their ways of living, their institutions, and their customs as they affect problems of military government; (*b*) lectures and assignments concerning recent major events and developments which explain the relation of the areas to the causes and the stakes of the war, and which explain the special political situations that the military government official must deal with.

The following represents kinds of subject matter which are called for in this part of the curriculum:

PLACE

The location of the region with reference to adjacent regions and why that location is significant.

Access to the area by roads, railroad, water, air; distinguishing features of transportation in the area.

Climate, temperature, rainfall, and some of the results which may be expected from extremes; the means for guarding against these results.

The soil of the area, whether covered or barren, types of crops, fertility, topography, altitudes, minerals.

Effects of technological changes on the natural resource base, such as cultivation for export, mining development, construction of railroads, airports, etc.

---

[12] Division Memorandum Training Circular No. 2, dated April 10, 1943, prepared by the Military Government Division, Office of the Provost Marshal General, Army Service Forces.

Water supply and its problems; irrigation.

General relation or effects of the presence or absence of natural resources upon food, dress, and activities of the people.

PEOPLE

The racial composition of the people of the area; where these races have come from.

Whether there is a movement of the population, from where and to where.

Analysis of birth and death rates and knowledge of resulting pressures; analysis of principal causes of death rates.

Linguistic, racial, religious, and other groupings; status and caste relations and some of the specific problems emerging.

Influence of the stronger social, racial, color, religious or other groups on domestic politics and on international relations; special points of friction which must be watched.

HOW THEY MAKE A LIVING

What the basic natural resources are and their extent.

The dominant industries and other economic activities based upon them.

Types of special skills and institutions based on dominant industries and kind of international trade.

Recent changes in the local economy resulting from technology, war, colonial policies, tariffs, etc.

The labor supply—its amount, skill, treatment, freedom, wage rates, organization, political activity; presence or absence of a labor movement.

The professional and managerial groups in the community—their size, recruitment, status, and influence.

The ownership of land, size of tracts, tenancy, terms of holding, changes in' holdings, peculiarities of land law.

Effect of government upon the daily life—taxation, public utilities and services, government ownership and regulation, government monopolies, subsidies, tariffs, social security.

Financial control within the community, banking groups, control by corporations, political effects (e. g., Japan), representation of foreign financial interests.

HOW THEY ARE GOVERNED

The presence or absence of colonial government.

The degree of local self-government and administration.

The positions, number and authority of local officials, their selection and their relation to central government. The subdivisions of government, organization, the relation of central and local units.

The role of elections, tradition or status in the selection of officials.

Political parties or groups, their types of organization and methods. Party programs, leaders and slogans, their racial and social foundations, their intensity of feeling.

The Civil Service, its selection and training, presence or absence of a spoils system; its status and influence in the community; its stability; the possibilities of its use in occupied zones.

Significant features of the judicial and legal systems, forms of punishment, authority of courts, etc.

Government finance, sources of revenue and principal objects of expenditure by local and central governments. Peculiar methods, forms and objects of taxation.

The role of invisible government; place of distinctive individuals and their leadership.

HOW DO THEY LIVE

The characteristics of family life and the resulting effects upon the community.

Religions and their social and political influence; religious influences affecting local life and customs, e. g., diet, ceremonies, the relation of the sexes, and the use of special places and objects of worship.

The schools and what they teach, general and technical; the control over the educational system.

The degree of literacy; the availability of popular education.

Reading habits, libraries, newspapers, magazines, radio.

Censorship and control of the press and education.

The major popular classics, other books.

The distinctive features of local architecture, arts, music, dress, sports, diet, etc.; special accomplishments in literature, arts, and sciences; accomplishments of particular pride.

Use of money, barter, wages, price understandings.

Sanitation and living conditions.

HISTORICAL BACKGROUND AND CONTEMPORARY WORLD AFFAIRS

The essentials of the historic relations of the area to other adjacent or related areas and to the United States.

The events, trends, and ideas leading to World War I.

The efforts at peace settlements; efforts toward international organization; international rivalries and other factors dominant between World War I and World War II.

Major current theories and ideologies; American and British theories of Democracy; Communism; Fascism; International Socialism.

2. Language Training

Officers who at time of assignment to training have speaking or reading ability in a foreign language useful in the area for which they are being prepared will be given continuation instruction in that language insofar as is feasible and to the extent required. All other officers will be given instruction in a language of major importance in the area for which they are being prepared; the language shall be one of the following: German,

Italian, French, Japanese, Malay, or Melanesian Pidgin. Where desirable and feasible, certain officers may be given continuation instruction in more than one language, or continuation instruction in one language and initial instruction in another.

All language instruction will be according to modern methods of intensive language training, making use of native speakers of the language unless these are unavailable.

3. *Special Application of Civilian Specialties to Military Government Situations*

The purpose of this instruction is to assure that the officers in training will appreciate the state of their respective sciences, professions or specialties in the area for which they are being prepared, and to give the officers practice in fitting their special competences into a comprehensive plan for meeting a situation which may later be encountered in the field.

It is likely that this objective will best be achieved by assigning teams of officers in training to the solution of assigned problems. In preparing solutions, officers in training will require the services of faculty members having competence in various fields of technical, professional, or other specialization.

This outline[13] presents a general idea of the type of knowledge which was considered essential for personnel assigned to military government duty and in general to any other duty which required a similar type of training. Given the broad aspects of the curriculum, how was the program to be effected?

The language phase was to be directed by the sponsors of the Intensive Language Program, a project of the American Council of Learned Societies, which for a number of years had carried on special programs or experiments concerning learning a language by intensive methods and by concentrating on the oral skills. On the other hand, the problem of area studies was not so easily solved. The Chief of the Military Government Division called in a number of experts representing a wide range of interests in the study of contemporary civilization, and the group finally worked out a standard curriculum for the study of foreign areas. These two programs were combined into one unit and the curriculum was adopted by the Director of the ASTD and distributed to colleges and universities in the spring of 1943 as the course of study to be pursued in the Foreign Area

---

[13] Two early curricula, Nos. 704 and 705, were established using this general statement as a basis. See Appendix B.

and Language Program of the ASTP. The colleges and universities giving these programs and the languages taught are listed in Appendix A.

The experiments which the American Council of Learned Societies had carried on had proved that languages could be learned quickly by the intensive method, and as the Army objective was to impart to the trainee a command of the colloquial spoken form of the language, this intensive method was adopted. Moreover, the intensive program, in concentrating on the oral approach, omitted much of the traditional impedimenta. Their programs were to insist on the fundamentals of the language and omit the refinements and embellishments of literature, get the student to think in the language he is studying and prevent him from translating it into the form of English to which he is accustomed, minimize grammar and syntax, and continue endlessly with drill repeated over and over again, small amounts at a time, until the materials are mastered.

For purposes of clarity and understanding, the Army directives, as issued on June 23, 1943, are quoted as follows:

Specific Objectives [14]

The objective of language instruction is to impart to the trainee a command of the colloquial spoken form of the language. This command includes the ability to speak the language fluently, accurately, and with an acceptable approximation to a native pronunciation. It also implies that the student will have a practically perfect auditory comprehension of the language as spoken by natives. Experience has shown that with the proper methodology, the objective can be achieved in six to nine months.

Study of the system of orthography in which the language is normally written is not an objective *per se*. It is to be undertaken only to implement the attainment of the above defined objectives. The time in the course at which written materials in the normal orthography of the language under study can be introduced will vary from language to language. It will be conditioned by the degree to which the system represents a phonetic transcription of the language, i.e., the degree to which the succession of written symbols represents the succession of the significant sounds in the speech stream. In Turkish and Hungarian such materials can be used from the beginning; in Japanese and Chinese only very late, if at all.

[14] Curriculum No. 71, Specific Objectives, Language Study. This is, however, a later edition.

Methodology

Any methodology which will achieve the objective outlined is acceptable. The following remarks are suggestive, not prescriptive. Provision is made in the curriculum for seventeen contact hours of language study. These can be effectively used in accordance with the following plan:

(*a*) One-hour demonstrations, five days a week, by the senior instructor of the course on the structure (pronunciation, grammar, syntax, word formation, etc.) of the language;

(*b*) Two-hour drill sessions, six days a week, in the presence of a drill-master who is a colloquial speaker of the language, preferably native born. Work in drill sessions is under supervision of the senior instructor who sees that it is keyed to demonstrations on structure.

The demonstrations on the structure of the language should be so planned that all the essential structural characteristics of the language will be presented during the course and in the order of difficulty which they constitute for the American learner. The supervised drill sessions should give the trainees protracted practice in the form of conversations which exemplify principles brought out in the immediately preceding demonstration on structure. They should further provide review drill on the material previously covered.

It is of crucial importance that the number of trainees in the supervised drill sessions be kept small. In no case should the number exceed ten. In general an instructional team will consist of:

(*a*) One senior instructor for each assignment of 80 men.

(*b*) Four drill-masters for each 80 men.

Under this arrangement the time of the senior instructor would be absorbed in offering the five demonstrations a week on structure and in supervising the drill-masters. Each drill-master would handle two two-hour sections of 10 men each per day. The drill-masters need not be trained teachers; their chief function is to speak their own language. With very brief training they can be taught to draw the men out and encourage them to practice on the limited materials with which they work in each session in accordance with the plan of the course. Care must be exercised to prevent the drill-masters from misinterpreting their function and assuming the role of teaching the structure of the language. This is properly taken care of in the demonstrations given by the senior instructor, and the drill sessions should be devoted entirely to practice.

As far as practicable, men studying the same language should be housed and messed together and otherwise encouraged to practice the language they are studying.

It is evident that reading and writing were to play a minimum role in this program.

LANGUAGE STUDY[15]

By comparison with the prewar college language course wherein reading skill was emphasized as the chief aim, the intensive language courses were to call for a much higher concentration of the student's time, preoccupation—at least in the early stages—with the spoken form of the language under study, and use of new materials prepared by the scientific linguists with special reference to the oral approach to language teaching.

Organization

One of the more striking features of the ASTP language and area program was the complete novelty of the undertaking, for, except as experiments, nowhere had such a program been envisaged before. On every campus where the program was in effect, a tremendous amount of organizing was necessary before the work could begin. As the Army was not always able to ascertain its exact needs in any one language, with the possible exception of Japanese and German in which the largest numbers were required, soldiers would sometimes arrive on certain dates and with vague Army instructions. The modern-language teachers were presented with an almost insurmountable problem. In nearly every case, new teachers had to be secured in order to handle the number of classes required by the increased hours of the intensive courses. In normal times two or three teachers were able to handle the language programs; now twice that number or three or four times that number were needed in each language. Refugees who never taught before were hired to act as informants and, under the guidance and supervision of the senior instructor, did creditably well. Only in a few instances were trainees called upon to act as informants to conduct the drill sessions.

Each language had a senior instructor in charge who arranged and planned the course, prepared or supervised the preparation of special material in the more exotic languages, and in some instances in the more traditional tongues, taught the grammar or

[15] "A Survey of Language Classes in the Army Specialized Training Program." Report of a special committee prepared for the Commission on Trends in Education of the MLA [New York].

analysis classes, controlled the work of the drill-masters, and prepared and administered examinations and tests. At nearly all the institutions the senior instructors were members of the regular teaching staff, were trained linguists and often not native speakers. On the other hand, in so far as possible, all drill-masters were native speakers of the language in question. It was customary for the drill-masters to be present during presentation of the grammar, and frequently the senior instructor observed or visited the drill sections. When this type of observation and supervision was an integral part of the curriculum, the program was nearly always better. In fact it has been stated that by far the most important single factor in the pronounced success of many of the programs was the close control exercised by the course supervisor, one of whose major assignments was to synchronize the work of the grammar classes with the work of the drill sessions.

At each institution a coordinator was at the head of the program. With the course directors, which varied in number from college to college, depending on the number of languages taught, the coordinator arranged the schedules of classes and examinations and integrated the work in area with the work in language instruction. Each institution, while it was aware of the Army directives and specifications, was left more or less to plan in its own way the minor details of organization, preparation of materials, and methods of presentation.

The drill-master, called upon to handle from eighteen to twenty-four (usually the number was twenty) drill hours per week, had a rather heavy burden especially when it is realized that this was nearly always oral work. This meant that he was in charge of two conversation groups of five to ten trainees during each of their six two-hour drill sessions per week. He would remain in charge sometimes throughout the term of twelve weeks, or there would be a shifting of drill-masters from one group to another which was true of some institutions. The drill-master was to serve as a model for the students whom they could imitate. He was supposed to use his native tongue, never English. In correcting errors he was to give only the correct usage, and not explain the grammatical problem involved. That was to be left to the grammar or analysis class. He was to confine himself to the vocabulary with which the student was familiar. It was his duty to conduct the class in such a way as to enable every student to get a chance to speak and to be patient with the awkward and halting expressions of the trainees in the early stages.

When the drill-masters followed to the letter the prepared material of the course, that is, did not dominate the conversation or exhibit their knowledge of English, both of which they were tempted to do and sometimes were actually guilty of doing, the students really progressed. Almost the entire burden of the two general directives of the Army—the ability to understand anything spoken by any native on any normal subject and the ability to speak the language with fluency and accuracy—rested upon the drill-master. It was his job to handle all the new material in the drill session in its endless repetitions, and to use the knowledge of the students, little as it was in the foreign tongue, in rephrasing the conversational material for further drill. Sometimes the drill-masters had an opportunity to give the trainees a part of their vast store of knowledge of their own country and travels. They often brought to their classes carefully prepared subjects for conversation, and thus maintained enthusiasm and interest.

Selection of trainees

The screening of the trainees generally took place in Specialized Training and Reassignment (STAR) units where their special abilities were determined, and from there they were sent to one of the fifty-five institutions offering area and language training.[16] The men were not always allowed to study the language of their choice and in some instances were forced to start another language when some groundwork had already been achieved in another one. The Army, however, recognized this as a mistake, for it was known that a student who had already begun in one language might do better if he were to continue in that language rather than start all over again in another. However, there was the feeling that ability in one language meant general

[16] "A History of the Army Specialized Training Program" (MS on file in Historical Division, War Department Special Staff), p. 55.

ability in others, and with the program of the intensive courses devised as it was, training in any language would be accomplished in six or nine months. Not too much concern was given to this problem. On the other hand, when trainees once assigned in any one language unit had had previous training with that language, they were placed in conversation groups ready for more advanced work. The beginners were given frequent tests to determine their respective abilities at various stages, so that they could be moved into fast or slow sections. The sectioning was often very carefully done, one of the institutions providing as many as twelve different levels.

In general the men selected had definite linguistic aptitude and were in some cases superior to the students at representative universities and colleges. Perhaps the basis of selection was responsible for this fact. Trainees for this course were selected from noncommissioned ranks, were twenty-two years of age, and had completed their basic military training. In addition to this, they had to qualify on three counts: (1) a score of 115, later raised to 135, in the Army General Classification Test, (2) demonstrated proficiency in foreign languages, and (3) completion of at least one year of college work.

Drill sessions

A brief word about the drill sessions may not be out of place here since it was in these classes, six times a week for two hours each day, that the trainees had a chance to practice the language. Drill classes were limited to ten students. Before them, the drill-master stands and reads at normal conversational speed a few questions and answers most of which are new to them, and therefore they have to listen attentively in order to understand them. After two or three such readings, aided by gestures, intonation, and facial expressions, the class repeats in chorus, sentence by sentence. Next, the printed version is passed out to the students, and the chorus work is repeated while all eyes follow the text. This lasts for about ten minutes. Then the class divides into two groups of five, and each begins its own repetition of the phrases and answers in regular order, mistakes and mispronunciations being corrected by members of the group.

This again lasts about ten minutes. Finally, the students put aside their papers and divide into five groups of two each. With key words placed on the blackboard, five separate dialogues are carried on in different parts of the room. The instructor moves about, listens to each group, corrects individuals if necessary, and then reshuffles them in different groups of two. For the next day, the drill class will be patterned more or less on the same lines except for a brief review of previously learned material at the beginning of the class hour.

The devices and techniques were many and varied, all based on imitation of a native speaker and aimed at the gradual ac- quisition of a large number of useful phrases and vocabulary. Repetition based on mimicry and memorization was a vital part of the process. In some instances, the students also wrote as they heard and pronounced, which had the advantage of a fourfold, instead of a threefold method of attack, and thus sound and spelling were associated from the beginning. In the later stages of development there were endless possibilities which gifted teachers used, such as impromptu dramatic situations or skits, "area" lectures in politics, economics, or other related subjects, quick paraphrasing of sight material, lectures by guest speakers from the local community, and even free discussions on some current and controversial topics—politics, religion, morals, war guilt, and so on. A little guiding by the teacher helped to keep the discussion varied and interesting.

Reading and writing

While the main objective of the language program was to teach the students to speak and to understand the foreign language, they did learn to read as well. Some teachers believed that the emphasis on speaking the language aided rather than hindered reading. The area study which the students followed along with their language study treated the contemporary his- tory, the geography, the economics, and in some slight degree the culture of the countries studied. As the books dealing with this material were not graded for English-speaking students but were written for the nationals of the various foreign coun- tries, the ability of the students to read such materials shows clearly a transfer from the ability to understand and speak to the ability to read.

Reading was introduced at various stages in the courses. It is not to be confused with translation, a great deal of which was done especially in the Oriental and Eastern European languages. Translation was freely used in some of the grammar classes when the limitations of time and the need for clarity required it.

Writing was not used at some institutions and was held to a minimum in nearly all cases. However, many students desired to write, and they often wrote down the foreign phrases which they were to learn orally. After all, writing, for some students, helps to fix more firmly the new phrase which they are to grasp and learn. Dictation of sentences and even paragraphs was used in the Western European language classes. Apparently any attempt to keep the language entirely oral was an impossibility. Sometimes dictations were given and the trainees' papers would be collected, corrected, and returned to the class the following day. Inasmuch as the program concentrated on oral work and review of already learned material plus the new assignment for the following day, no attempt was made to go over the corrected dictations; and, as the students barely glanced at their papers, all the possible benefits of this feature were likely to be lost.

Grammar

With respect to grammar, it is well to recall the passage dealing with this feature in the general Army directive presented above, namely, that one-hour demonstrations, three days a week, by the senior instructor of the course were to be given on the structure (pronunciation, grammar, syntax, word-formation, etc.) of the language, and that the supervised drill sessions were to give the trainees intensive practice in the form of conversations exemplifying the principles brought out in this demonstration on structure which were to precede immediately the drill sessions. Many variations from the traditional procedure with respect to the presentation of grammar were brought into play and much new experimentation was tried. This involved the local preparation of a great variety of new materials and the oral presentation of them. The amount of time spent on developing new material varied with the language; and, in the case of the Oriental languages where texts were almost completely unavailable, the entire course had to be prepared locally.

There were, of course, the texts prepared by the Armed Forces Institute in the more common Western European languages. These were modeled after the plan and technique of the so-called scientific linguists. There were also texts of the more rare Oriental and Eastern European languages prepared by the American Council of Learned Societies. However, many of these were not available until after the close of the ASTP program.

Most teachers conducted the grammar session in the foreign language as early as possible, some from the very first day. Various types of presentation were used: conventional grammar texts that made extensive use of the foreign language, teaching of grammar by induction and analysis of carefully prepared drill sentences, and structural analysis of dictated passages. In general, an attempt was made, especially in the case of carefully prepared drill sentences which were "type" sentences embodying a grammatical rule, to teach grammar functionally, that is, by actual use in a sentence in the foreign language. This was done by starting with the simplest form of a complete sentence and adding to it. The sentence became by degrees an elaborate statement, which would include the grammar point to be learned.

As no formal grammar was planned for use in the course, students had to secure their own review grammars or construct their own from what was presented to them in the demonstrations on structure by copying down the grammatical rules and principles presented orally. An effort was made to exclude grammatical explanations from the drill sessions because all explanations of grammatical phenomena really belonged in the grammar session. To do this, two types of possibilities existed: either the grammar involved in the model sentences could be explained before the sentences were introduced into the drill sessions where they were to be committed to memory, or the grammatical content could be explained after these model sentences had actually been memorized in the drill session. Best results seem to have been achieved when the drill sessions were geared to the subject of the grammar session.

Preparation for these intensive language courses was limited to the grammar sessions, as it was felt that little or no time need be spent on the material which was supposed to be memorized in the drill sessions. If no outside preparation were required, then the total number of hours spent on the language excluding area study, was eighteen or twenty. This seems to be a far cry from the original plan of the Intensive Language Program sponsored by the American Council of Learned Societies, which defines the intensive course as one which occupies the full time of the student, generally computed at about fifteen hours of classroom instruction, fifteen hours of drill with native speakers, and from twenty to thirty hours of individual preparation per week. Some of the institutions provided drill-masters or instructors to assist the trainees in their preparation during supervised study hours.

Vocabulary

A suitable vocabulary for these intensive language courses was another problem, especially a vocabulary geared to the oral approach. The frequency lists in the Western European languages were considered by some teachers to be based upon literary content and therefore were thought to have little place in an oral course which emphasizes practicality of vocabulary. Many local lists were prepared as a substitute for these frequency word lists which were generally topical in scope, were centered upon everyday needs and experiences, and formed a basis for conversation. The design of the Army-sponsored texts was such that new words for the most part were to be learned from their use in short phrases or sentences rather than as detached words in a vocabulary list. In general, the total vocabulary of these texts was about 1,500 words.

Inasmuch as these texts were called *Spoken French, Basic Course* or *Spoken Chinese, Basic Course* the concept of what constitutes basic vocabulary for a language is brought to the fore. Whether or not anything was achieved in the matter of establishing either generally or specifically a basic vocabulary in any of the languages taught in the ASTP is still not known. Much exploring and experimentation in this field yet remains to be done. In the CATS program, topical word lists and phrases were presented in technical manuals prepared by the Army which were related to tasks that would confront the trainees in the performance of their duties as engineers, lawyers, doctors, and other professions in occupied territory.

Training aids

The ASTP language program was supplemented in varying degrees, depending upon facilities available and the locality of the institution, by the use of mechanical devices and by promotion of extracurricular activities carried on in the foreign language. Because they were made available by the Army, these mechanical devices were put to a much wider use in the program than was the case in the traditional prewar college curriculum.

Extensive use was made of the phonograph for both listening and recording. The use of commercially prepared recordings was widespread inasmuch as many of the trainees owned their own sets, but these were not considered to be of any great value since there was often no topical or textual connection between them and other course materials. Transcriptions of short-wave broadcasts and March of Time recordings were made available, and these were good for the more advanced students because of the variability of the contents, their timeliness, and the general relationship to topics under discussion. Again, the recordings that were made to accompany the language guides and the basic language courses were available in large quantities.[17] These were considered an improvement over most language recording sets because they were provided with pauses during which the student could repeat immediately the phrases spoken on the records. Such a device carries the student beyond mere passive listening. These recordings can be a real aid to the teacher and perhaps even supplant him for brief periods,

---

[17] For some languages, neither the basic language texts nor the recordings were available until after the close of some of the ASTP programs.

since this is more or less what he does when he furnishes the phrases and the students repeat after him. However, these are best used for study periods, or self-instruction, for there is no advantage gained by having recordings replace a native speaker when one is available.

A great many benefits are derived from recording machines when drill-masters cut their own records containing lesson materials. These are then available for repeated aural review, either optional or obligatory. When students make their own recordings in the foreign tongue, at properly spaced intervals, they can measure, by a careful diagnosis of their speech faults, progress or improvement in pronunciation. Machines and discs should be of high-grade material and there must be first-class acoustical conditions. Some slight use was made of the radio and the telephone as other audio aids.

A widely used aid was the moving picture, especially commercial films. These were either secured by the institution or supplied by the Army through surveys made for them through OSS, the Office of Alien Property Custodian, the Museum of Modern Art, and the various branches of the Army. Unless these films are acoustically perfect, comprehension is extremely difficult, and for beginners, of practically no value. An interesting technique reported on the use of films was the case of one instructor who provided the spectators in advance with a synopsis of the story and at twenty-minute intervals had the film stopped for five minutes to permit questions. In another instance, the film was first shown in the afternoon, and after a drill session in which the film provided the subject of conversation, a second showing was held in the evening. For the most part, films were shown in the evening and, since attendance was not compulsory and no control was provided, no direct gain or value was ever measured.

For outside activities there were lectures given by foreign visitors speaking their native tongue, informal soirees arranged by staff members or local residents who spoke the language, local club-meetings, meals in foreign-language restaurants, cinemas, and church services. The staging of original playlets in the foreign language was widespread among the trainees; in some institutions they even edited their own newspaper in mimeographed form. Singing was very popular, and in some colleges a special hour once a week was devoted to an organized singing session at which songs were learned by heart. Language tables were provided in the mess halls and were helpful, especially when staff members made it a practice to be present.

In some instances, in accordance with the Army directive, trainees were quartered by language groups, an arrangement which promoted additional use of the language. Where students learning the same language were quartered together and language tables were provided, there existed a system comparable to the language houses which have for a long time been an integral part of the traditional language program. Here one sees again, as was more clearly seen in the case of the Navy language program, the idea and the partial existence at least of the educational concept of the "planned environment." Whether a language house is really a planned environment depends largely upon the facilities available and the use to which those facilities are put. For the Army and especially for the Navy, the idea of a planned environment was a possibility. It merely remained for the directors involved to determine whether or not the idea would be realized.

Texts prepared for the ASTP in language study follow:

Spoken	Burmese	Spoken	Japanese
"	Chinese	"	Korean
"	Danish	"	Malay
"	Dutch	"	Norwegian
"	French	"	Portuguese
"	German	"	Russian
"	Greek	"	Serbo-Croatian
"	Hindustani	"	Spanish
"	Hungarian	"	Thai
"	Italian	"	Turkish

AREA STUDY[18]

The Foreign Area and Language Program of the ASTP was so planned that both area and language should provide

[18] Especially helpful for this section have been various foreign area and language curricula; and William N. Fenton, *Reports on Area Studies in American Universities.* (Washington: Ethnogeographic Board, Smithsonian Institution, 1945.)

complementary disciplines, one for the other. They ought, therefore, to be envisaged in the light of a single self-composed unit, not as separate fields of endeavor. However, both language and area have enough distinctive features about them to be considered as separate fields of interest without losing their special relationship. Language study for the most part was to occupy fifteen out of a total twenty-five-hour program, and area study ten hours; the ratio between these two fields was nearly always the same in the various programs. Since the trainees in these early programs were to be assigned to the same type of military duty, that is, to military government functions, a knowledge of the language and of the situations that obtain in a foreign area was of great significance, for it was believed that personnel so assigned could not possibly operate effectively in such a capacity without this form of training.

We have described above the need for civil affairs officers in occupied territory to handle the thousand and one specialized problems that arise in the administration of occupied territory. The need was equally great for personnel not of officer rank to assist these civil affairs officers. While the administrative officers themselves were all men who were well-known and who had had long years of experience in their specialized fields as lawyers, health experts, engineers, and so on, they were not men who had received any particular or even general knowledge of the foreign area, wherever it was to be. They were, therefore, not able to transfer their specialized knowledge to any possible area to which they might be assigned. The Civil Affairs Training School (CATS) program was devised to assist them in making this transfer. Equally true, the men who were trained in the ASTP Foreign Area and Language Program had not had any training in this field at all, so for them the program and the training that it provided was a new experience.

The CATS program and the Foreign Area and Language Program of the ASTP were similar since both called for language and area study. The Foreign Area and Language Program was scheduled to require six to nine months, while the CATS program required but three months for completion in the European areas (later reduced to two months) and six months for completion in the Asiatic areas. Both programs adopted the intensive methods of language teaching, and both programs had a similar interest in area studies, but on different levels. The men assigned to the ASTP were to receive a broad basic training in their chosen areas, so that they could understand and assist in the solution of whatever problems should confront them, while the men assigned to the CATS were to be trained in the actual handling and solution of these problems. It will be seen, then, that while the programs were similar, there were none the less certain fundamental differences.

Again, the selection and assignment of personnel to the two programs was different. The men assigned to the ASTP program, in addition to the regular requirements for entrance into all the ASTP curricula, were required to show a special aptitude for language study. On the other hand, the personnel assigned to the CATS program were required to have had both training and experience in the specialized fields relating to public administration and government and therefore they were older, more mature men for whom the ASTP language and area program would have been insufficient and unsuitable. Another essential difference was the fact that while both groups required in most cases a basic knowledge of the language in order to understand and speak it, the personnel assigned to the CATS program required additional and specially prepared vocabulary lists relating to the respective fields of public administration.

Another feature in the matter of assignment of personnel once the course was finished provides a further reason for the differences in the programs. All the men in the CATS programs were to be assigned, upon completion of their training, to military government duty. While the program of area and language study in the ASTP was created at the request of the Provost Marshal General's Office and the desired curriculum was proposed by that office, not all the trainees upon completion of the course were to be assigned to that branch. Other branches of the services, when they learned of the program, established quotas to fulfill their expected needs from the ranks of the ASTP trainees. Men were trained in area and language studies under the ASTP for duty with all arms of the Army Ground Forces, and for duty with the Army Air Forces, Military Intelligence Service, Office of the Provost Marshal General, and the Signal Corps in the following approximate percentages:

Army Air Forces..............................	3%
Signal Corps.................................	10%
Office of the Provost Marshal General............	10%
Military Intelligence Service...................	19%
Army Ground Forces.........................	58%
Total	100%

In every instance, however, it was expected that graduates of the ASTP area and language program would be assigned to duty requiring use of their knowledge of the foreign language and area. For the most part they were to be trained for combat duties in which their language facility and general areal knowledge would be of extreme importance. In smaller numbers they were to be trained for administrative, policy-making positions.[19]

With the requests for these new quotas of men made upon the ASTP by other branches of the services, it was necessary to revise the program of language and area study to meet the increased number of trainees representing this wider range of interests. Consequently Curriculum No. 71 was established to supersede Curricula Nos. 704 and 705.[20] The modifications incorporated in the new curriculum were very slight. There was a change in the number of contact hours required for each subject. Rather than treat geography, history, and contemporary institutions in sequence throughout a period of three terms, "Area Study" and "Contemporary History, 1914 to the Present," were listed as separate subject-matter offerings to continue throughout the three terms. In the new curriculum no further provision was made for the classes in "Police Science and Law Enforcement," listed in Curriculum No. 705, which was prepared especially for the ASTP to meet the needs of the Office of the Provost Marshal General.

[19] Curriculum No. 71, Foreign Area and Language Studies, General Objectives of the Curriculum.
[20] See Appendix B.

The language study for these curricula has already been discussed, as well as the relationship of language to area. It was a case of relating the history, the geography, and the customs of the area to the language under study, with the expectation that the one would aid the other, especially when, in advanced classes, area study would be conducted in the foreign tongue.

Since all branches of the services were making demands on the ASTP for their respective quotas of personnel in area and language, the new Curriculum No. 71, established to replace the earlier ones which were originally planned for military government purposes, is of special significance because it was more or less the final form of the prescriptive program for the colleges and universities which were responsible for its successful operation.

The objectives of the ASTP area study were to be met by the use of course content which logically would fall into three general categories:

    I. Geographical study
    II. Historical study
    III. The study of contemporary institutions and culture

The materials included in these categories could be treated concurrently in an integrated program running throughout the three terms of the course, or they could be treated in any sequential order which the institution believed to be desirable.[21] The following series of check lists relating to the three categories listed above are quoted verbatim as it is believed that inclusion of these lists as prepared by the Army is the best way to show in detail the numerous unrelated factual items which the trainees had to make their property. These items are unrelated only as factual items; they are intricately interrelated as they combine to give the total picture of a contemporary culture. One must always bear in mind that these areal studies were constantly being related to the general framework of American civilization by way of contrast or as a means of vivifying the exposition by virtue of the differences that obviously would prevail.

[21] Curriculum No. 71, Specific Objectives. Area Study: AST 265-66-67.

AREA STUDY CHECK LIST I [22]

Geographical

1. Climate, both average and extreme. Human adaptation to climate.

2. Landforms, with special reference to military terrain features.

3. The relation of water supply to landforms, lakes, streams, rivers, and sea coasts. Water networks and directions of flow; navigability. Artificial manipulation of water supply. Human needs in the area and requisite military water discipline.

4. Vegetation of the area. Utilization for sustenance (types of edibles and non-edible fruits and plants), shelter (both civilian and military), and general economy. The effect of vegetation on the movement and distribution of population. Has the student seen graphic representation (movies, slides, etc.) of vegetation in the area, its appearance in the military landscape?

5. Types of animal life: draft, food, and fur-bearing. Reptiles: harmful and harmless. Insect life and relation to epidemiology. Fishes, seafood, and fish oil.

6. Natural resources; exploitation and use in peacetime and under military control. Degree of economic self-sufficiency. Relation of critical products to problems of military supply in the region or area.

7. Accessibility of the region or area from contiguous regions; in terms of foot and mounted travel, vehicular, water, and air traffic.

8. Logistics; routes of travel and communications, with particular attention to strategic points in the military network. Distances and spatial relationships of the area in terms of distances and spaces known to the trainee.

9. Ethnic origins and survivals. Identification of ethnic characteristics in the region or area.

10. Linguistic origins and survivals. Identification of linguistic groups and variations in the region or area.

11. Movements of the indigenous population resultant from seasonal migration, economic pressure, and military exigencies. Periodic migrations between the region or area and adjacent regions.

12. Has the trainee a knowledge of the types of maps prepared and used in the region or area? The chief points of difference between the indigenous system of mapping and surveying and that of the United States; symbols, scales, etc. Quick methods of orientation in the region or area itself.

[22] Curriculum No. 71, Specific Objectives; Area Study: AST 265-66-67-68. Three check lists were provided as a series of suggestions for those institutions offering an area and language program.

Area Study Check List II

Historical

1. Does the trainee understand the significance of the historic slogans in common usage in the area, e.g., Liberté, Egalité, Fraternité? Mare Nostrum?
2. Historic chronology of events of importance; understanding of historic "periods" in the past of the particular area. Anniversaries of historic events and their celebration.
3. Racial movements through the area and the historic consequences.
4. Growth of national (or particularistic and separatist) sentiment and political organization. Remnants of earlier political organisms still extant.
5. Historic boundary questions and rivalries; treaties and dates. Periods of expansion and periods of defeat and political submergence.
6. Development of common religion and religious institutions; the role of such heresies as are still extant; the historic reasons for common religious taboos or customs.
7. Important changes or "revolutions" in the technological, commercial, industrial, and agrarian history of the area.
8. The historic development of existing legal and governmental forms and institutions.
9. The history of important cultural, economic, and political contacts with regions outside of the given area, and reciprocal reactions; historic alliances and diplomatic alignments.
10. Evidences of liberal ideas and institutions; historic prototypes of the "Four Freedoms" in the area.
11. Military history, famous battles, and wartime heroines. Popular concepts as to the reasons wars were won or lost.
12. "Great" historical figures; particular biographical knowledge of contemporary leaders in the area.
13. Periods of cultural greatness and dominance; survivals and current memories of the same.
14. The sustained sequence and narration of events in the area from the eve of World War I to the present.
15. Historic problems of the area not yet solved; ambitions (social, political, geographical, etc.) not yet realized.

Area Study Check List III

Contemporary Institutions and Culture

1. Does the trainee have a usable knowledge of the vital statistics of the area (and those of the surrounding region which may affect the area); age groupings; death rates and leading causes of death?

2. State of public health and sanitation; epidemic diseases (particularly those of military significance, such as venereal disease, typhus, malaria, etc.) ; social conventions in relation to the control of disease.
3. Food and drinking habits.
4. Types of dress and relation to climate.
5. Types of dwellings; furniture; conventional types of village or city lay-outs.
6. Folk ways; taboos and conventions (particularly those bearing on religion or family and sexual relationships).
7. Types of religions, institutions, and beliefs; the role of religion in everyday life; place of the clergy or priesthood.
8. Social status groups and caste systems (with special emphasis on those stratifications of society inimical to each other) ; revolutionary or "underground" movements.
9. Economic relations of classes of society; the manner in which each gains a living; types of prosperity; methods of finance.
10. Current conditions of factory life and labor in general; existing degree of technology in industry, agriculture, etc.
11. Impact of local government on daily life (with a thorough knowledge of local government organizations and the services rendered) ; the judicial and police systems.
12. Relations between local government agencies and higher authority; elements of friction.
13. Relations between the civilian population and the armed forces of the area; military service laws, etc.
14. Education; degree of literacy in the area; extra-curricular education by means of youth organizations, etc.
15. Public information facilities and types of government control.
16. Popular amusements and sports.
17. Some knowledge of popular literature, as well as language classics.

These check lists were intended only as a series of suggestions relating to those items of information which should be the property of the trainee when he had completed the course. It was anticipated that the teaching facilities of each institution would find much to be added. It was believed that these detailed lists of factual material should aid in developing the understanding of the trainee and enable him to observe and classify rather than to develop his powers of memorization. Military experience had shown that the ability to analyze and understand properly a situation arising in a foreign area is more important than the possession of a collection of facts concerning the area which easily might prove to be irrelevant and soon out of date.

For teaching and administrative purposes two major regions, Europe and Asia, were designated for general instruction, and for obvious reasons. It was hoped that the approach to the study of the area should be from the general European or Asiatic area to the more specific and particularized region in which the individual language is normally used. However, it was left to the institution to determine the details of area definition with reference to the combination of languages and language areas taught therein. It was hoped that each institution would urge the individual teachers to organize and conduct the classroom sessions in such a way that the trainee would see a definite connection between what he was learning in the classroom and his probable future duties as a soldier.

Special emphasis was placed on the fact that this program was not to be in any sense of the term a revision of the social science courses presented under the guise of area study. New methods of instruction had, therefore, to be devised to meet the objectives entailed in the area study curriculum.

Desired organization [23]

A special faculty group in each institution was to be designated to develop and plan the details of the program. This group was to include one member at least from each of the following departments: languages, anthropology, sociology, history, economics, geography, political science, or any others which might conceivably have an interest in the several disciplines which would constitute the core in the general integration of areal studies. This would mean a new contribution to educational practices and procedures, since the successful planning and operation of such a course of studies would necessarily require to a very marked degree a sense of interdepartmental cooperation, both in the spirit of the term and in the letter.

It was expected that within the framework of the curriculum outlined each institution would utilize any special facilities, personnel, or knowledge available. A special reference room in the

[23] *Ibid.*

college library would be established for the use of area and language trainees. In this connection, extensive use would be made of case methods, museum material, appropriate films, government reports, and travel and geography material. Comparative treatment of this material should be employed throughout to relate the American background to the people and area under consideration. In this venture, it was hoped that the respective institutions offering this program would cooperate in the preparation of new instructional material and in the exchange of any material so prepared. The exchange of materials, ideas, and personnel would tend to encourage rather than hinder the best use of all specially qualified personnel and assure that reasonable comparability would be maintained in the execution of the curriculum in area study.

As the period of historical study was designed to explain existing institutions, events, and controversies in an area which, only a few weeks ago, may have been little more than a name to the trainee, an antiquarian and excessively academic approach was to be avoided. Emphasis, even in the historical aspect of areal study, was to be on a contemporaneous basis. The instructors had the dual task of teaching the history of the language area and the adjacent regions with a proper concern for the facts, they had to inform the trainees fully as to the interpretation of history and of the specific historic events and problems commonly taught and accepted in the area itself.

The most difficult problem of the areal study program, perhaps, was that dealing with the contemporary institutions and the general culture of the area under study. No teaching materials were available and no techniques had been developed for this type of course. Materials may have existed for an isolated and separate discipline such as history, but it was necessary to bring all these scattered materials of the several isolated disciplines together and correlate them for actual use in the classroom on a workable basis. This necessitated close cooperation on the part of those involved in the participating subject-matter specialties. An attempt had to be made to submerge the interest of the special and separate discipline involved in favor of the more general welfare of the program. Here was an opportunity to study an area, or region, in terms of its totality rather than in the light of one phase of it, such as geography or any of the other participating disciplines.

The special course in Curriculum No. 71 entitled "Contemporary History, 1914 to the Present" specified as its objectives that it should give the trainee an understanding and an appreciation of the scope and importance of the war in which he was engaged as a soldier as well as some knowledge of the events leading up to and conditioning the course of that war; and that it should heighten morale and lend interest and motivation to work in the other phases of the area and language program.[24]

The problem of periodization in contemporary history is not only a difficult one, but it is also a debatable one. However, the period from 1914 to the present was chosen arbitrarily as a segment of history which conformed most readily to the teaching time available and which would admit proper background treatment for events occurring in the immediate past and present. Since experience had indicated that the average trainee assigned to the ASTP maintained an intelligent and continuing interest in contemporary events, this course, two hours a week, should serve to meet a very real need. Each institution was allowed to make such chronological and topical divisions in this arbitrarily chosen period as seemed feasible. It was believed that emphasis should be given to events as current as those chronicled in the morning paper and to military history since the outbreak of World War II. This course in contemporary history was to be global in character, but emphasis was to be placed on Europe or Asia, as indicated by the group of languages and areas studied in the particular institution.

Area study in the several institutions

Such were in general the broad outlines of the organization of the area study program and its course content. How were each of the institutions to weld together into one program of study the heretofore isolated disciplines? How were they to transmit this imposing body of facts to the trainees so that the completed program would represent a definite sense of unity

[24] Curriculum No. 71, Contemporary History, 1914 to the Present, AST-201-2-3.

and cohesion? After all, the significant knowledge about foreign peoples and the way they live is scattered through a dozen academic disciplines.   However, educators did grasp the challenge to bring together a group of faculty men who reorganized and pooled their knowledge in the effort to explain the important items about a place, a people, and a culture.

In general, it can be assumed that the same type of confusion prevailed on every campus while the program was in process of organization. Because of their location in large metropolitan centers, some schools had advantages over others both with respect to facilities and personnel.

Some institutions began making plans for the future program that they would operate upon receipt of notice that their institution was to be one offering an area and language program. In one of these early attempts to define the program, a faculty group had already decided that area study was not history, economics, political science, geography, or sociology, or any other academic subject then offered in the colleges. Nor was it a combination of all of these. It was rather a type of regionalism which demands a realistic rather than an academic organization of knowledge. For this reason it must treat the man of the area in his entirety in a way impossible in academic subjects. This attempt at forecasting the needs of area study was focused in the right direction, at one university at least, from the very beginning in spite of the obstacles encountered later.[25]

There were several methods employed in presenting the substantive aspects that combine to depict a civilization or a culture. One of the methods—that of concurrent courses, each on a different aspect of the area, geography, history, or economics— was suggested by the Army in the general outline of its program. Each of these was to be given by a specialist. Another was the block system which attempted to bring all of these aspects together in one course with the material presented in successive blocks in geography, then history, and then economics, each treated separately for scheduled periods of time throughout the

[25] Thomas A. Brady and A. J. Stankowski, *The Foreign Area and Language Study at the University of Missouri. The University of Missouri Bulletin, XLVI* (July 20, 1945), Arts and Science Series No. 2.

nine-month program. Integration of this material was left to be very much a function of the student, whether spontaneous or not. A third type of approach was that which presented the area in a single course, with integration being a matter of concerted effort on the part of the faculty.

To achieve any degree of success in a completely integrated areal program, a planning committee, including both administrative officers and members of the staff, was essential. This committee not only planned the program but also exercised a continuing and corporate supervision over its entire progress. The committee would have to plan the sequence of the lectures so that the story could unfold in the most effective manner. The participating faculty members attended one another's lectures, a practice which was of incalculable value in the successive revisions of the course. New techniques of presentation were employed such as the *panel discussion* in which a group of staff members or outside specialists would draw out the implications and interrelations of previous lectures or present a topic of controversial character; the *interview* technique, in which an informant (usually a native or any person familiar with the area but not necessarily the particular problem) was questioned by a member of the staff, usually on the basis of a rehearsed outline; the *project* technique in which a number of student members, operating as a team, focused knowledge drawn from several disciplines upon a single problem.

Any system of integration had to seek machinery which would make possible the pooling of approaches of the various social sciences in illuminating the institutional life and structure of the foreign area under examination. For example, Japanese rural society, instead of being treated only from the special point of view of the sociologist or the anthropologist as in the traditional approach, was also analyzed by a political scientist in terms of its political structure and by an economist in terms of its economic organization and problems. With this combined attack of sociologist, anthropologist, economist, and political scientist, the result naturally ought to be a richer and better-rounded understanding of Japanese rural society. This system provided interrelations between political, economic, and social problems, or evoked new ideas which might remain obscure or completely forgotten under the traditional approach. Attention was actually called to issues often ignored in the traditional course which followed one discipline at a time. Again participants, both teachers and students, derived mutual benefits.

Interdisciplinary collaboration, while present, was limited of course, due to the speed with which the programs were put together and their operation. Cooperation was necessary, but it was affected by the exigencies of the war; and while timely and perhaps even adequate, cooperation was not always wholly genuine. Some men preferred to remain in their own fields in which they were pre-eminent while others cooperated wholeheartedly and believed they gained by the experience.

It is to be remembered that the material as organized in the curriculum for area study was grouped realistically and not academically. In the section under the general rubric of how the foreign people make a living, some of the material would fall into the academic field known as economics and some in the field of political science. The same admixture of material from the academic point of view was found in the general field of how a foreign people is governed. Here, it may be remarked that it is the fields that are artificial and not the material.

With respect to the final group of suggested topics (Area Check List III), that dealing with how a foreign people lives, there was present material considered proper for several different academic fields. Some of the material in certain sections was of a type familiar to men trained in history, government, and economics, while other material closely allied to it belonged primarily in the field of the specialists in literature and art. Because of this interrelation and admixture of items of knowledge in the several fields, an attempt was made at one university to rearrange this material so as to fit more nearly the academic specialty in which the teacher was trained so that he could manage it and would not be beyond his depth.

In this reorganization of the material, there were several phases of the intimate life of the area which were assigned to the language teachers to be used as material in the instruction of the language classes. No attempt was made, of course, in this rearrangement to change the essential content of the areal curriculum. It was primarily a case of sorting the informational items and parceling them out to the specialists whose task was to present them to the trainees.

An attempt was made, as previously stated, to integrate the material into a broad mosaic so that the trainees would acquire at least a general idea of the nature of the country to which they were going and something about the people and their way of life. This does not mean that integration was always complete or genuine. To learn to view a certain problem or institution within a foreign country from various angles—to look at it in the light of as many academic disciplines as possible—ought to be a profitable experience for the trainees. Whether or not the individual trainee made the necessary synthesis to view the problem in its entirety rather than in the light of a separate discipline was a problem which the trainee reserved for himself. The course provided for the integration of the several disciplines, and the program directors for the most part saw to it that the lectures and seminars were planned on an integrated basis. In this connection one very good method of integration concerned the relating of a problem in a foreign country to a similar one in a culture with which the men were intimately acquainted, usually their own. There was some advantage to this since the greatly divergent experience and social background of the members of any given class very often led to interesting and profitable discussions.

The greatest problem on any campus was one of cooperation between the various departments, once it was understood by the course directors what the Army directives were. The attempt to integrate the material of the course almost made it imperative for the various faculty members to cooperate. The establishment of the area or regional program can be considered in general to have been an attempt to counteract the extreme departmentalization which is characteristic of the present educational system. This element of intense departmentalization, quite unlike the Middle Ages when a single discipline like religion was the core about which all learning centered, has existed for a considerable period of time and is a phenomenon apparent in all educational levels. There have been attempts in some colleges and universities, such as St. John's and the University of Chicago, to counteract the tendency toward departmental segmentation.

Whether this interdepartmental cooperation evidenced in the area study program has left anything in the way of a permanent fixture within the various faculties is a matter of doubt, since some institutions already are experiencing the trend back to prewar segmentation. The foreign-area programs, while valuable and essentially sound from the Army's point of view, were short-lived and bore the stamp of an experiment. As in all experiments, whatever values may accrue are somewhat lost sight of unless there is recurring use of them and continuous building-up of evidence in their behalf.

While the idea of an "area" or "regional" type of study is not new, the programs were highly successful in view of the objectives that were outlined for them. What is new are the methods and the techniques involved; that is, the combination of language with area study and that to the exclusion of all other learning, the concentrated hours of contact with the study, the pooling of knowledge and personnel, the integration of material into one body and under one heading, and the emphasis always placed on the contemporaneous aspect of the area rather than the past.

Again the various programs in several universities under the general heading of School of International Affairs bear a resemblance to this idea, but these are distinctly different in that they may concern an area as large as the world, and the subject-matter courses which make up the program of studies are pursued separately and often consecutively. Any cross-fertilization that may exist is primarily incidental and certainly not planned, even if intended. Again the approach is usually not from the slant of the contemporaneous scene which, in the light of the times in which we live, is one of the more important aspects of the wartime area-study program. A knowledge of the present scene within a given area may place one in a position to foresee many of the moves before they have become *faits accomplis* having repercussions which affect other areas for good or ill.

Classical civilization has long been the object of broad and intensive study, but its problems were far less complex than those of modern society and in some periods lent themselves to synthesis by a single investigator.　In fact, some educators have suggested that a combination of courses such as the area and language program of the Army based on a modern cultural region might replace the old and fast-disappearing series of programs centered about classical civilization.　These older programs had much to offer in content, discipline, and wisdom, and were tempered by those high moral principles which were part and parcel, if not the core, of the programs.[26]

[26] *Ibid.*

VI. THE CIVIL AFFAIRS TRAINING SCHOOLS PROGRAM

THE SCHOOL of Military Government at Charlottesville with its limited facilities was unable to handle the total number of Civil Affairs personnel deemed necessary to satisfy the needs of the War Department in its program of military government in occupied territory.

It was early revealed that the number of personnel required would be around 6,000. This personnel was to be secured in the following manner:[1]

(a) By increasing the training groups at the School of Military Government from 100 to 150, there could be trained by close of the year 1944............................ 1,000

(b) By training 100 officers per month at a company officers school at the PMG's School, Fort Oglethorpe, Georgia (later Fort Custer, Michigan).................... 2,400

(c) By commissioning from civil life certain experts in professional and technical skills and training them in a combined military and university setup................. 2,500
                                                                     ———
    Total 5,900

The School of Military Government at Charlottesville was originally expected to train a limited number of staff officers for positions in civil affairs headquarters. On the other hand, the CATS programs operating in civilian universities were to train officers in civil affairs who would serve for the most part in field positions. Within the military government establishment itself this difference in later assignment of the trainees within the respective programs created divergencies in the curricula of the two types of schools.

At Charlottesville there was little or no language study, and foreign-area study was definitely subordinated to other instruction. For the Civil Affairs Training Schools, language and area comprised almost the whole curriculum, with military

[1] "History of Training, Military Government" (MS on file in Historical Division, War Department Special Staff), p. 12.

government somewhat in the background. Although the military government program was essentially a "training" program in the military sense, it was in large part based upon subject matter normally encountered in academic curricula. One of the primary objectives was the indoctrination of officers in the institutions, customs, and languages of many political and geographic areas throughout the world. The approaches to that part of the instruction were a combination of history, economics, political science, and modern anthropology. Consequently, the Provost Marshal General's Division turned to civilian institutions for the establishment and operation of this program.

To train these experts listed under (c) above, who were to be commissioned directly from civil life,[2] was the task of the Civil Affairs Training Schools which were established in ten universities for the European and Asiatic theaters. Harvard, Yale, Pittsburgh, Michigan, Stanford, Chicago, Boston, Northwestern, Wisconsin, and Western Reserve were to establish programs for the European and Mediterranean areas. Six of these universities—Harvard, Yale, Michigan, Chicago, Northwestern, and Stanford—were also to establish programs for the Far Eastern area.

THE TRAINING SETUP

The training of these officers falls into three main categories.[3] Part I, referring to the general principles of military government, was to be taught in a course at Fort Custer, Michigan; Part II, concerning the study of backgrounds, including the languages of the various areas of possible occupation; and Part III, concerning the problem of tying together Parts I and II, were to be the content of instruction at schools established in civilian universities.

Four distinct fields of instruction were determined in this curriculum to which the trainees would turn after the month's

[2] Authority granted 12 October 1942, by WD letter AG 320.2 (9-23-42), P R-A-SPGAO.
[3] "History of Training, Military Government," op. cit., p. 38.

preliminary training in the Specialists Officers Course at Fort Custer. These were language, instruction in area characteristics and conditions, military government, and military training and physical exercise.[4] Of these four fields of instruction, language and area are of concern to this study because of the close relationship to the same program, but on a different level, in the ASTP.

Language instruction was to follow more or less the same methods and use the same techniques as were employed in the ASTP Foreign Area and Language Program.[5] This type of language instruction was considered best since, in the selection of officers, previous language knowledge was subordinated to administrative, professional, and technical skills, and therefore the majority of the trainees chosen for their professional skills were lacking in language background. Language study was to embody maximum proficiency in speaking and understanding the spoken colloquial language and to supply an elementary knowledge of the written language sufficient to enable officers to follow simple printed instructions such as street signs and time tables, at least for Japanese.

With respect to area instruction,[6] the general objective was to supply the officers with knowledge which would enable them to anticipate conditions and situations, and meet with understanding and confidence the problems to be encountered in the foreign area. There were to be area lectures dealing essentially with the people of the area under examination, their economic system, political setup, ambitions, international perspective, and the special problems involved in the occupation of the area. These were to be supplemented and strengthened by area conferences involving the actual solution of hypothetical problems organized about Civil Affairs teams, specialty groups, or any appropriate grouping of officers which would utilize all the pertinent skills. Motion picture films, demonstrations, and exhibits appropriate to the area were also to be considered.

[4] *Ibid.,* p. 42.
[5] *Ibid.,* p. 47.
[6] *Ibid.,* pp. 47–48.

A typical outline of the subjects of area lectures relating to the Far East follows:

SUBJECTS OF AREA LECTURES [7]

1. Geography of the Far East
2. The Japanese People: National Character and Political and Social Organization
   a. Origins and Historical Perspectives
   b. National, Political, and Social Structure
   c. Village and Town Life
   d. Religion
   e. Cultural Patterns and Social Attitudes
3. The Japanese Economic System
   a. Introduction: Principal Features of Japanese Economy
   b. Population Problems
   c. Agricultural Problems
   d. Industrial Problems
   e. Labor
   f. Transportation Problems
   g. Domestic Trade
   h. Monetary and Fiscal Problems
   i. Social Welfare and Social Insurance
   j. International Economic Relations
   k. Summary and Outlook
4. Special Problems Involved in Occupation of Japan
   a. Introduction to Problems of Military Occupation with Reference to Japan
   b. Military Currency
   c. Price Control and Rationing
   d. Exchange Control
   e. Banking in Occupied Areas
   f. Government Finance and Taxation in Occupied Areas
   g. Control of Industry
   h. Social Welfare and Social Insurance
5. Japanese Occupation Techniques
6. Historical Background and International Situation
   a. Introduction
   b. Japan's Foreign Relations: The Problem and Its Setting
   c. Highlights of Japanese History
   d. Japan, China, and the World
   e. Contemporary Developments

[7] From *Curriculum, Far East Program*, University of Chicago, 15 June 1944. Civil Affairs Training Program, Office of the Provost Marshal General.

It is apparent from this outline that the interests of the CATS program reveal a different emphasis from that which was placed on the area program for the ASTP. The officers trained in the CATS program were more mature than the enlisted men in the ASTP, and many of them had records of genuine achievement in their professions and callings. Consequently, the area instruction in the CATS program resulted in much more emphasis on the industrial, commercial, and professional aspects of the area than was true in the ASTP.

At each university, a member of the faculty was constituted Director of the Civil Affairs Training School on its campus. Under this director, a substantial civilian faculty operated in each university, supplemented by numbers of occasional lectures and consultants drawn from all available sources. The Provost Marshal General furnished each university an Army officer, usually a colonel, and a graduate of the School of Military Government, who acted as a liaison officer and was designated Associate Director. Under this officer there were varying numbers of military instructors who were Army officers with some military government training. The liaison officer was charged specifically with the responsibility of coordinating with the civilian director the activities of both the civilian and military sections of each CATS faculty. The Provost Marshal General was able to achieve a desirable degree of uniformity throughout the several CATS programs through this liaison officer who was under his immediate jurisdiction.[8]

GENERAL PATTERN OF TRAINING

In the beginning, the university programs were experimental to a considerable degree, for modifications and improvements were constantly occurring. Some of the features that prevailed in the instruction at the School of Military Government were taken over bodily and adopted in the CATS programs, particularly the organization of Civil Affairs teams and the use of military government problems as teaching devices. After much experimentation and with the completion of the first two or three

[8] "History of Training, Military Government," op. cit., p. 43.

classes, a more or less standard curriculum was adopted, varying of course slightly from one program to another. The procedures described below came to be the prescribed pattern:

To the work in languages,[9] for students destined for the European area, were allocated 120 to 136 contact hours during two months, at least 80 of which were devoted to conversational drill sessions with no more than eight officers to the class. For the Asiatic area,[10] 476 contact hours were allotted, at least 392 of which would consist of conversational drill sessions of not more than eight officers.

To the area lectures 48 to 62 contact hours were allotted; at least 36 were devoted to Germany and Austria, distributed as follows: 6 hours on the political system; 10 on government, with major emphasis on local government organization and services; 4 on law, law enforcement, and the judicial system; 10 on the economic system; 3 on public health and welfare; and 3 on education propaganda, press, and radio. For the Asiatic area, an allotment of 248 contact hours was made; 200 hours were to be devoted to area lectures, 36 hours to area conferences, and 12 hours to motion picture films or other demonstrations and exhibits.

From the beginning, the Provost Marshal General's Office insisted that instruction should be under control of a director who would correlate all parts of the instruction and shape them into a single integrated course. At most CATS, the director was able to set up a faculty group to plan instruction and develop materials for a period several weeks prior to the arrival of officers for training. Where this was done, a degree of integration was attained and there was little overlapping of lectures. Faculty members were assigned lectures which under normal conditions they would not have given, since even prepared lectures were actually revised at the insistence of the director or his committee.[11]

While the lecture method succeeded well for the younger and less mature trainees of the ASTP, this was not true for the more

[9] For European area, *Ibid.*, p. 45.
[10] For Asiatic area, *Curriculum, Far East Program*, University of Chicago, 15 January 1944.
[11] "History of Training, Military Government," *op. cit.*, p. 47.

mature and experienced men assigned to the CATS programs. The lecture method of instruction, while it was successful in some instances, was supplemented by the use of other approaches. Some of these were the use of military government problems, panel discussions, area conferences, use of informants who were cognizant of the area, nationality contacts especially in the metropolitan centers, and utilization in some cases of the trainees' knowledge.

The content of area instruction was similar to that outlined for the ASTP Foreign Area and Language Program, already discussed in an earlier portion dealing with that curriculum. However, the trainees assigned to the CATS programs, already equipped with training and long years of experience in their chosen skills, were not interested primarily in area study as such. They thought they knew how to deal with whatever problems should confront them, especially within their special fields, because of what they already knew. Consequently, for them some means had to be devised to show them how to transfer the knowledge of these special skills which they had exhibited in an area with which they were intimately acquainted to one which was foreign to them.[12]

In order to demonstrate the relevance of area instruction for these trainees, it was found necessary to organize them into Civil Affairs teams for the solution of assigned military government problems. These teams consisted ordinarily of from ten to fifteen officers representing different grades and different backgrounds of training and experience. The military government problem described a situation which the officers might expect to encounter in the field and required for its solution preparation of a plan of action, organization, and procedures which the team would recommend for adoption. By use of these problems a great deal of information about the area was presented, since without knowledge of certain aspects of the area the problem could not be tackled. The military government problem convinced the officers that instruction in area was useful, and it became a helpful guide to the faculty, since it revealed in what

[12] *Ibid.,* p. 48 *et seq.*

type of instruction the group was weak, and consequently enabled the faculty to plan instruction systematically for the area.[13]

The ten universities participating in this program were given wide discretion in fixing the method and content of instruction; they all used the Army's outline of basic knowledge which was to become the property of the trainees upon completion of the course. The several directors enjoyed varying degrees of success in their efforts to mold the instruction into a compact course of study. That some faculty members, who were eminent in their respective fields, were obliged to give lectures which they might not voluntarily have given, and that proposed lectures were revised at the insistence of the director or his committee were features of the program that required fullest cooperation. The deviations from customary academic practice were justified in a two- or three-month training program designed to fulfill Army needs.

At bottom, the Civil Affairs Training Program represented, like the ASTP, an experiment in cooperation between the War Department and the several universities involved. It was a case of the War Department delegating to the universities a function which it believed they could do better because the several institutions were already functioning organizations and the War Department would have had to start from the beginning. That the training programs prescribed by the War Department should have succeeded in the various institutions without too much friction and achieved the desired objectives is attributable to the patriotism of the institutions and their willingness to accommodate their normal peacetime approaches to the exigencies of war.[14]

Of great practical use in the Civil Affairs program were the Civil Affairs handbooks, of which seventeen were issued on each country of primary interest as follows: (1) Geographical and Social Background, (2) Government and Administration, (3) Legal Affairs, (4) Government Finance, (5) Money and Banking, (6) Natural Resources, (7) Agriculture, (8) Industry and Commerce, (9) Labor, (10) Public Works and Utili-

[13] *Ibid.,* p. 52.
[14] *Ibid.,* p. 54.

ties, (11) Transportation Systems, (12) Communications, (13) Public Health and Sanitation, (14) Public Safety, (15) Education, (16) Public Welfare, and (17) Cultural Institutions. The full series was published on Italy, France, Germany, and Japan. Some of them were prepared on Austria, Belgium, Denmark, Holland, Norway, and the Philippines.

Part Two

CURRENT EFFECTS IN COLLEGES AND SCHOOLS

VII. IMPLEMENTATION AT THE COLLEGE LEVEL

VARIOUS LANGUAGE journals, and in particular the *German Quarterly*, have devoted considerable space to an explanation of the language programs now in operation in the several schools reported on, which are modeled after the language programs of the armed services. Each of these reports relates to one specific language, such as German or French.[1] While these reports treating in great detail the several programs described are of value as they concern the particular language under examination, they do not reveal the over-all status of language teaching, especially in the light of the armed services programs where all the languages were supposed to follow a like methodology.

It was considered advisable to obtain an over-all view of language teaching relating to the wartime programs by getting firsthand information through direct visits to a selected group of colleges and universities to determine if there were programs in operation similar to those established by the armed services. This was considered desirable for two reasons: first, because, in those institutions where there are separate language departments, what one department might be doing would not be true of another; and second, because, if there were any carry-over values in the armed services programs, they ought to be reflected in the teaching of the several languages, including both Oriental and the traditional West European languages, rather than in a single language.

The information which follows, as a result of these visits and observations, has a particular significance with respect to intensive programs. While it was believed that intensive courses could not be integrated into the already overloaded college curriculum, the fact remains that a degree of intensiveness has been achieved without creating too great an unbalance in the total

[1] See, for example, *German Quarterly*, XIX (January 1946), 98; also, *French Review*, May 1945.

college curriculum.   The emphasis on the oral skills—the distinctive feature of the armed services programs—plays a very large part in these programs, also.   For the most part it will be seen that the programs relate to the elementary stages of language learning.

Concern over transfer from the first-year oral program to the second-year reading program has forced some institutions to modify somewhat the wartime language methods and procedures in order to meet this problem.

INTENSIVE BEGINNING COURSES

There are intensive courses at Institution A for beginning French, Spanish, German, Italian, and Russian. These courses came into being as the result of experiments which had shown the value of adopting them in the curriculum.   The traditional language class met three hours per week, and the regular accepted outside preparation was required.

The modern language department secured permission to offer these beginning courses, calling for no additional homework but for seven contact hours per week—three class sessions about twice the normal size and four drill sessions in groups of ten students each.   It was recommended that this feature become a permanent program of the university for beginning classes, with the specific recommendation added that the experimentation be allowed to continue with selected students at such times as might seem favorable with combined intermediate double courses of not more than twelve or not less than ten hours per week.

The entire group of beginning students taking French, German, or Spanish, met together—fifty, sixty, or seventy in one large room—for explanation of the daily assignment.   Here the foreign language is the rule, although a complicated grammatical point may have to be explained in English.   The teacher who conducts these three weekly grammar classes is one who knows thoroughly the structure of the language, the grammar, and the syntax and all the pertinent difficulties.   Ample opportunity is afforded the students to ask questions about matters which are puzzling to them.   An explanation is made with examples of the case in point, placed on the blackboard if necessary.

Later, with hours scheduled as for regular classes, the students are divided into groups of no more than ten, sometimes less, for drill in aural comprehension and oral expression. The drill sessions present a wide polarity of possibilities depending on the type of text in use, and vary of course with the teachers. One drill session in French repeated over and over with different examples used of expressions such as *un autre, encore un, quelqu'un,* and *n'importe qui.* A drill session in Spanish on the use of the subjunctive in noun, adjectival, and adverbial clauses brought forth numerous examples in point with the rule for the sequence of sentences being properly applied. Use of English in the drill sessions is forbidden except to explain or clarify a point of grammar which could not obviously be made clear if explained in the foreign tongue. In one drill session in German, numerous repetitions of the principal parts of verbs were given, both the strong and the weak. Variety was achieved by the use of many verbs and the formation of simple sentences in which they were used. Numerous questions were asked in German which the students must have understood, as eventually the correct answer would always be found. In another drill class in German, there were singular and plural forms of nouns to learn and case endings, taken at random from the reading or the conversational element supplied in the text. No one seemed harassed or hurried, no one was bored or not paying attention, for in a small class of this type every student is called upon to recite often.

In all the drill sessions there was an *esprit de camaraderie* between the students and the teacher, and there was an apparent fondness for the language that is somehow not always manifest in the traditional courses. In one drill session in Spanish, there was a brief session when every student was sent to the board to write exercises supplied by the teacher. The students were all at work at the same time, and when correction was made of the material on the blackboard, the students performed their own correcting. Only in classes as small as this is it possible for all students to be at the blackboard at the same time.

In the drill sessions, the reading would be done either by the teacher or the students, sometimes alternately, and numerous questions based on the text would be asked as the reading progressed. The students would answer them in the foreign tongue. In nearly all cases the first student called upon could answer. There was not any question in any class visited that could not be answered by some student. There was no necessity for translating into English, even though the question may have required rephrasing.

Other techniques observed as part and parcel of the drill session with not a word spoken in English were the giving of dictations and brief oral quizzes. Conversation was carried on between groups of two, in a Spanish drill session; first the prepared formula of the text is used, and then the groups proceed to a rehearsal or repetition of the same without benefit of the text. In such a case the student has by this very repetition learned by heart the conversation passage.

The drill classes seem to be an aid to the student, and he seems to enjoy them in spite of the fact that he receives no credit for these extra hours. The total credit allowed for the student's seven contact hours is three. There is also a definite carry-over from the recitation classes to the drill session in spite of the fact that they come sometimes on different days due to the difficulty in the scheduling of classes. For specially gifted students, for which there are two drill classes per week instead of four, the department arranged for a change of instructor on different days, thus giving students the benefit of different voices in the language and a variation of technique.

The grading of the students is the responsibility of the so-called senior-instructor, the teacher in charge of the course. He has the students under his tutelage for one or two drill hours per week in addition to the three recitations which he guides. It can thus be assumed that he has a controlling interest in the students though they come under the tutelage of others for some of the drill sessions. The alertness of the students, even in a large class of sixty or seventy, and the response made, show that such classes are possible as the Army pointed out, but they should not be the rule. The control of the students in these large classes is a problem, and certainly there does not and cannot exist the same abandon, the same *esprit de camaraderie,* as prevails in the smaller drill sessions. The department is aware of this and hopes soon to divide these large classes into two groups for this very reason.

The program seems to be succeeding, the students are enthusiastic, and the teachers are in unanimous approval of the value of both the idea of learning a language on the intensive basis and the use of the oral approach, which combines reading and some writing with emphasis always being placed on aural comprehension and oral expression.

It is interesting to point out that, whereas an instructor was in charge of one of the intensive courses as well as were higher ranking members, there were assistant and associate professors as well as instructors actually conducting the drill sessions. The department believes in, and the university has approved of, the program even to the extent that more teachers may be required and an additional expense will thus be created.

DOUBLE COURSES

Institution B has adopted intensive language classes, using the oral approach. However, in this college, the intensive elementary courses are not open to all beginning students in the languages. The intensive courses are open to a limited number of beginning students in French, German, and Russian. There was not a sufficient number of students registering for the elementary intensive Spanish class, and consequently none was scheduled. With respect to the elementary intensive Russian class, there exists no traditional type of course in Russian as is true for the regular language classes, and it is possible for this reason that the elementary intensive Russian class will have more prestige in and by itself for continuance since it will have no traditions or conservative measures to counteract. There will be no opposing forces to work against it. For the other intensive courses, there still exist the regular language classes which run parallel with them, and hence some friction may arise because of the conflicting opinions and the divided interests which attach to such a situation.

The elementary intensive classes have ten contact hours per week and offer the credit that would normally accrue for two courses since this intensive class is actually a "double course."

There are six drill hour periods, and four recitation periods for the elementary French class. For Russian and German the division is slightly different; there are eight drill-hour periods and two recitation periods, called respectively "practice" and "analysis." Though the major emphasis is on oral expression and aural comprehension, some attention is paid to reading and writing, since the students enrolled in these classes will continue with the specified language program of the college.

The students in the elementary intensive French class receive instruction four times a week on the general structure of the language, its intricacies and grammatical difficulties, and then meet in sections of eight students for six hours for drill sessions in the language. The drill classes observed were conversing rather freely with the teacher. There were also dialogues in French between two students on purchasing a ring at the jewelers; between two other students about purchasing a hat at the hatters. A third bit of conversation went on, several students continuing where the first student left off concerning a trip around the world and the necessary preparations connected therewith. The teacher supplied the words and phrases which were not known by the students or which they could not remember, and made the necessary grammatical corrections as well as those in pronunciation. There were only two outbursts by students into English, at which moment the drill-master would say, *"Pas d'anglais."* The drill sessions meet three times weekly for two hours each session with a brief intermission of ten minutes about halfway during the period, depending on what is being done at the time.

In addition, provision is made for students in this intensive course to listen to recordings of the lessons, done by the senior instructor on the sound-scriber apparatus. Arrangements are made for three weekly periods of one and a half hours each for this practice, but attendance is not compulsory. The teacher feels the students are progressing nicely.

For German, a quite similar situation exists. The students in the intensive course meet two hours a week for analysis on the structure of the language, syntax, grammar, and explanation of the new lesson and then are divided into small sections of about ten for drill. The drill session of the German class of ten students which was observed was conducted by a drill-master who was rather active both in talking and in gesticulating, thus more or less acting out the situations. There was constant questioning on the part of the teacher, with different students responding. Not a word of English was ever spoken in the class while under observation. The students were required to repeat often, and their mistakes in grammar or word choice were constantly corrected. The teacher later asked students to put various questions to other students, calling them by name for the answer. There was not too great an emphasis placed on perfect pronunciation in German, and though perfect diction in the language may have suffered somewhat, there were, so the department felt, compensating gains in better grammar, and in increase of vocabulary. German type is not introduced to the students until the second term of the intensive course, and a bit of reading is done in German with German type the latter half of the second semester.

Though the phonetic transcription which derives from the linguistic scientists is still used in the German class for the first eight weeks, and students are required to be able to write it, there is less adherence to the more specialized terminology of the linguistic scientists. Little or no use is made of recordings in the German classes.

For Russian a like story prevails except that the class is smaller and, being more or less new to the campus, is not hampered in any way by the effects of other methods, since this is the only beginning course in Russian. The material is all mimeographed or typed. Here again only a drill session was observed. The seven students and the teacher continued for one solid hour of one of their two-hour drill sessions without a word of English. These students meet for two one-hour classes a week for analysis of the language, its structure, intricacies, and difficulties, at which time a new lesson is introduced. There are then four hours of drill for each lesson begun in an analysis period. During the drill period observed, the teacher who is a Russian followed his text as did the students and required answers to the numerous questions put to them. There were endless repetitions of verb forms as the teacher went around the class again and again and always in the same order. Later with books put aside, the teacher asked students questions on where they lived, the time of day, and the like, with the students responding. The students apparently seemed to be understanding and enjoying the work, for many a smile would appear and an occasional burst of laughter would come forth.

AT A COLLEGE FOR WOMEN

Institution C, one of the larger eastern colleges for women, has also adopted a program of intensive courses on the elementary level. The college offers two experimental language courses— one in German, the other in Russian—patterned after or influenced by the army intensive courses. The elementary intensive German class meets nine times a week, three hours for grammar lectures and six hours for drill and the class is open to anyone beginning German. Various members of the department assist in instructing the class. The entire group of about forty is broken down into two groups for grammar explanation and into smaller groups for drill. Almost immediately the students are taught to read the German type, for, while more effort is put on the attainment of oral ability, reading and grammar are a very vital part of the course. Emphasis is placed on all three— speaking, reading, and writing—and in that order.

The German class follows the regular phonetic transcriptions if used, and the traditional spelling from the start. The teacher in charge felt that to learn any added symbols was an unnecessary burden to the students. As for any grammar terminology other than the traditional, the teacher also did not feel that such could be of any value in a language like German which has a well-defined literature and a definite, inflected written form.

For the most part, the oral drill concerns learning sentence patterns, either long or short, by rote. This procedure gives the student a few useful ready-made phrases and helps him acquire a feeling for the construction of the sentence and the word order, which has no connection with English word order. There were no specially prepared mimeographed materials since the class began using a conversational text at the outset. The course carries six credits.

For Russian, which also meets nine hours a week, the case is somewhat different. The class meets always as a whole, as the group is made up of only nine or ten, and there are no analysis or practice periods as such. The work progresses using alternately both techniques when the occasion arises in the same class period. The teacher, who had experience with the ASTP, does not believe that anything is to be gained by such a division for the class in Russian. While emphasis is placed on the oral approach, reading and writing begin as soon as possible and rather early in the course. Because no suitable book is available, the teacher at present prepares from day to day the new material, grammar and vocabulary, which the class is to learn. This material may finally be worked into a Russian text. No use whatever is made of the Army phonemic transcriptions, nor is any use made of the special terminology of the linguistic scientists. The method is apparently one of the teacher's own making and is patterned after the Russian classes which the teacher has given for nearly twenty years. This course also carries six credit hours.

For French, there is no experimental intensive course, as the teacher in charge believes that the existing six-hour course, on a less intensive basis, is sufficient for the small size of the class. Normally there are but five or six students entering the college who register for beginning French. This year, however, there are more, and if the number should increase materially, an intensive course like the German and Russian ones may be introduced. However, emphasis is placed on the oral approach; in fact, the students do not get any reading at all for the first three weeks, and grammar is taught functionally or inductively and not from stated rules.

There are no grammar analysis classes as such, and no drill classes as such; however, various members of the department assist in instructing the class. A specialist in the science of phonetics meets the class once a week for improvement in pronunciation. A recording machine is sometimes used which reproduces the student's voice so that mistakes in pronunciation can be heard.

As no formal book is introduced in the early stages, the

material varies from day to day, and the students themselves sometimes make up the material that they are to study. This is done rather ingeniously by the teacher asking questions about objects in the room for which answers are given in French. On one occasion, the teacher asked the students what they did when they went to the library, how they got in, what they did once they were in, and so on, and little by little the class formed a story which the teacher pieced together before them. Later it was typed and was given back to them in the form of a dictation. The story was in the present tense, and another day the same story would be given using the past indefinite tense which the students had been told was the conversational tense for past action. The teacher plans to vary the course, using different techniques from year to year, but always insisting on oral use of the language.

There is a special incentive for language study at the college— the language houses where the students reside and enjoy the atmosphere of a home. When the students live in one of these houses (it is obligatory, though they are not forced to sign pledges), they really work harder. Though there is no Russian house as yet, there is on the other hand a very comfortable and attractive Russian center where the students and teachers can convene for informal parties. Classes in Russian are also held sometimes in the lounge rather than the regular classroom when practicable.

Again, the students in German are looking forward to the day when the junior-year-abroad idea will be resumed and they can go to Zurich if they qualify. Several students have this in mind. It is natural that to meet these requirements, those of the language houses, and those for the junior year abroad, great stress must be placed on the oral approach.

It should be added that the students are required to spend in study, for the intensive courses, as much time in hours as the class meets per week.

FIVE-YEAR EXPERIMENT

At Institution D, there are intensive courses in Chinese, German, and Russian. However, in the fall of 1946, a new program was to be inaugurated on a five-year experimental basis, incorporating all of the ASTP language features. The Russian classes continue on the same intensive basis as they did during the operation of the ASTP language program, in that there are twelve contact hours per week and twelve credits obtain for this type of course. The Slavic department has its own method of instruction based on the oral approach. However, no use is made of phonemic transcriptions or any uncommon grammatical terminology. No distinct separation is made between analysis and practice periods. Emphasis is placed on oral expression and aural comprehension. Reading and writing are stressed early in the course. The language is taught intensively as it is the desire of the department to have the student making use of the language as soon as possible in the literature courses; or, if he is majoring in area, then in the related area subjects.

Chinese is patterned after the so-called "Army method," and operates in the same manner as did the Army language classes. The teacher is extremely proficient in the Chinese language and believes in the method by which he was trained and which he now advocates. He is concerned somewhat by the large numbers of hours that are devoted to language study, and suggested that there may be a "saturation point" beyond which a student cannot go effectively. He thinks that the fifteen and sometimes twenty or more hours that were utilized by the Army for language instruction were too many. He thinks nine or ten hours a week a better choice, depending, of course, on the student.

There are two intensive courses in Chinese offered, an elementary class and an intermediate class. The dialect taught is northern Mandarin. There are three hours of grammar analysis per week when the entire group of beginning students meets together, and five hours of drill per week with the group broken down into sections of five students each, under a Chinese tutor. For the intermediate course, there is a total of eight contact hours per week, with two hours of grammar analysis and six hours of drill. It is the plan of the Chinese department to place no more than five students whenever possible, in a drill session, thus making the student-teacher ratio one to five. The material to be studied and learned is prepared and mimeographed on a day-by-day basis, and the load of the teacher under this *modus operandi* is heavier than usual. Apparently, new types of material constantly in a state of flux is the rule, at least until a good standard book is available for Chinese instruction.

The manner of presenting new material is along the line of pattern or type sentences, beginning with the shortest possible complete sentence and adding to this original sentence until a longer one is formed. In each case, the lengthened sentence, including the final one, is a complete sentence, and explains a thought or idea all the way from its crudest form to a very elaborate one. At the basis of this elaborate sentence, there still remains easily discernible the original simple sentence from which the expanded form grew. These sentences are learned by heart by various means of repetition.

No attempt is made to enter area study until the language is mastered and can, therefore, be used in area courses.

The proposed plan, introduced in the fall of 1946, is reported because of its relation to the present program and its close analogy to the ASTP pattern for language instruction. It is to be noted, however, that what is contemplated in the early stages may represent in no way at all the final setup when all plans have been worked out and these are stated in concrete terms on paper. No plans as definite as this are yet available.

The present language requirement is eighteen credit hours in a language, which would normally require three years to complete, provided no doubling of courses was permitted and only one three-hour course was taken each semester. It is proposed to introduce a language program which will satisfy this requirement in one year, nine hours of study being devoted to the language each semester. There will be two large departments, and all the language instruction will be grouped together into one department. Likewise, all the literature courses in all languages will be grouped together into one department.

This plan, of course, involves considerable change, since there will be no German department, no Chinese department, no romance language or Slavic language department as such. All courses will be grouped together into two departments, the modern language department, and the modern literature department.

For instruction in the language, all entering students will follow the intensive method of instruction. There will be secured a specialist in this method to head the language department who will guide the experiment during its five-year existence.

If a student enters having already had some language instruction, he will be given a proficiency examination to determine his status in the intensive language program; that is, if he has a high rating he may enter the second term of the intensive course.

PARALLEL OFFERINGS

At Institution E, a rather full program of intensive courses runs parallel with the program of traditional courses. In addition to the intensive language courses, there is offered a series of literature courses for those students who have taken the elementary intensive courses in which instruction follows the oral approach. These literature courses likewise parallel the traditional type literature courses. A further distinctive feature is the continuance of the program now in its third year with courses running through the junior year. It is planned to inaugurate a similar type of course for the senior year, so that eventually a full four-year program of intensive oral courses, language and literature, will exist side by side with the traditional four-year language-literature program.

The number of contact hours per week varies in this intensive sequence. For the elementary intensive courses there are nine contact hours per week (six credits), and for the second and third year intensive courses, four contact hours per week (four credits). Though emphasis is placed primarily on the oral approach, with reading and writing a vital part of the intensive program—for French, Spanish, and Russian—there are divisions into analysis and drill for the elementary intensive courses only.

There exists also an intermediate intensive course for students who offer two or three entrance units in French or Spanish. This class meets three times a week for training in aural comprehension and the use of the spoken language, and three times a week for oral practice with a native instructor. The students who complete this course successfully are then eligible to continue in the literature courses in the intensive oral sequence. This course carries six credits.

Since there are almost completely full programs in both intensive and traditional types of classes, not all students are allowed to take the intensive courses. Through a process of selection, the students are weeded out so that only exceptionally good students are allowed to enter the intensive series.

The German department is likewise planning an intensive series of courses, though the elementary intensive course is currently the only one in operation. It meets nine hours per week, with three hours of analysis and six hours of conversational drill. There is, in addition, an intermediate intensive course which meets six hours per week for freshmen who offer two or three entrance units in German, as is true for French and Spanish.

The romance language department hopes soon to introduce an intensive program for the teaching of Portuguese, if and when the number of students increases enough to make the program a possibility.

A number of classes were observed in every language and on every level, and instruction was entirely in the foreign language. In one Russian class, where a drill session was involved, the students, apparently without being forewarned, were all told to go to the board for a dictation in Russian. When correction was made by the teacher, it was noticed that very few mistakes were made, and there was none made by one student. This was an elementary Russian class. In a French class during a drill session period, there was drill on verb forms among other related grammatical content, and the class was conducted entirely in French. The students had previously learned the grammatical terms in French during the first two weeks of the term when some English was allowed. In an advanced Spanish class the students were required to tell stories one by one before the class, based on some personal incident like the loss of an article. Seven or eight students spoke more freely before the group in Spanish than some students normally do in English, their native tongue. One student spoke fluently and without a grammatical mistake.

A COMPOSITE METHOD

Institution F makes use of the oral approach though courses are really not intensive. Reading and writing are introduced in the first meeting of the class. For the romance language department, during the past twenty-five years, this has been the situation. French, Spanish, and Italian follow more or less the same pattern. Special texts that lend themselves to use of the oral approach have been prepared by members of the department for classroom instruction. Classes meet five times weekly and a total of five credits is given for the beginning courses.

Here a plan is in operation which develops the skills of speaking, comprehension, reading, and writing as correlated or coordinating skills and not as isolated abilities, since it is believed that one aids another. For this plan which comprises several methods and various techniques, special graduated texts are required with specially chosen vocabulary and content leading from simple, easily understood statements to more difficult and thought-provoking passages. The students are led gradually step by step. For oral work, they begin with short, simple statements and work up to lengthy, smooth-running and harmonious passages which are repeated in unison before being transcribed in written form, when corrections in spelling and grammar are made. Great emphasis is laid on the use of the blackboard. In fact, all the language classrooms are provided with sufficient blackboard space so that every student—classes average twenty-five students—may be at the board at the same time.

The department attempts to present the material to be learned in such a way that every pupil is engaged actively and is mentally alert for the complete class period. This is achieved by various means, perhaps the most important of which is the continued use of the foreign language at the normal rate of speed. In dictation, no attempt is made to slow down for the laggard, since he either understands what is being said or he does not. There are no halfway measures. The students are aware of this at the beginning of their courses in foreign language instruction and must adapt themselves accordingly. Grammar is taught more or less functionally, and a vocabulary is built up by firsthand association with the word, in its use in a sentence rather than by learning special vocabulary lists by rote or by translation. There is no translation. The use of a large number of cognate words in the beginning of the text introduces the student immediately to the foreign language in terms that he can understand without translating. An important element in the preparation of the texts, aside from the use of cognate words, is the choice of material which is allied through historical or geographical relationships, either directly or remotely, to the student's past knowledge. The material must also take the student, because of the situations chosen, into the foreign atmosphere, at least in spirit. The material again must have a sequence arrangement involved which is so natural and logical that the student is enabled to follow fairly long passages or to remember without actually memorizing them.

The following are samples of the case in point:

Au huitième siècle les Arabes ont traversé le détroit de Gibraltar, l'Espagne, et les Pyrénées pour envahir le midi de la France. Ils avaient déjà pris la ville de Bordeaux et ils étaient dans la vallée de la Loire, mais Charles Martel, qui était le maire du Palais à cette époque, les a battus à la bataille de Poitiers et ils sont retournés en Espagne, ou ils sont restés jusqu'à la découverte de l'Amérique en 1492.

Or this:

En el otoño las pájaros de esta región van al sur para pasar el invierno cerca del Golfo de Mejico donde hace mas calor; pero en la primavera vuelven al norte para pasar el verano cerca de los Lagos Grandes donde hace menos calor.

The above examples contain a rhythmic flow or harmony that enables the student to recall readily a fairly long passage apparently without actually passing through the normal phases involved in rote memory. The writing of part of the passage quoted, based on knowledge already acquired by some other means, because of this logical and rhythmic arrangement seems to make it easier for the student to continue writing the entire passage. One student remarked that in this type of technique the fact helps to remember the language and the language helps to remember the fact.

In nearly all classes observed, especially the elementary classes, there were individual compositions put on the board by every student. While the writing is being done, the teacher moves about the room and corrects mistakes which he sees as he passes along. It may be that he cannot correct every detail at the board, but at least he has every student busily engaged in writing the foreign language and has been able to bring to each individual student some grammatical error which he has corrected. In several instances there were cases of long passages similar to those quoted above which were given at normal speed to the class. The class would recite in unison the passage and then were told to write it on the board. Corrections, if necessary, would be made individually as the teacher went from pupil to pupil, and finally correction would be done collectively. When all students had completely written and completely corrected passages, all would erase and begin again a new passage. Here were cases where oral expression, aural comprehension, writing, and reading were all more or less simultaneous, at least as much so as is possible in such a situation. Grammar, vocabulary, history, and geography all became elements of the material with which the student was dealing. In all classes, elementary, intermediary, and advanced, questions were asked in the foreign language and the students were required to answer in the foreign tongue.

In one Spanish class the following techniques were part of the first half-hour of the class session, which ran so smoothly that one had the feeling it was a natural and common occurrence. First, the students were sent to the board where each was required to put a question in Spanish; this done, the students were told to move two places to the right and correct the question for form, grammar, and spelling, and then answer it. Again, the students were told to put a verb form in Spanish, any form, on the board and then they were told to move one place to the right and use the verb in a correctly written Spanish sentence. After this the teacher asked questions in Spanish, the answers for which the students would write on the board. Long numbers would be called out rapidly and the students would have to put the number on the board in figures. Again the teacher would make up long sentences which the students would first repeat in unison. Then, in some cases an individual student would write the statement on the board. Such practice is all done rapidly and the students do not become lost or flustered. The passages contain for the most part material with which the students are familiar, with but a little new material added so that progress, in spite of what may seem repetitions, is made. This assembling of new material with material with which the student is already familiar may go on endlessly without tiring or boring the student, since the variations achieved by adding new words or ideas change the content. In this way what is drill of the first order is not thought of as drill.

The department feels that endless drill on one minute grammatical point used repeatedly in sentence after sentence eventually defeats its own purpose, and thus it has faced the question squarely: Is there not a point reached beyond which drill does not aid the learning processes, but actually becomes a hindrance? This attitude resulting in a newer technique provides a challenge to the students and they seem to like it.

There is a great deal of observing in all classes by members of the department and there is undoubtedly much gained in the process. All the beginning classes are controlled by a senior member of the department who feels free to interrupt any class and carry on without any loss of time to the class or disturbance to the students.

There is a rather heavy language requirement at the university in the Arts College, generally equivalent to a reading or working knowledge of a foreign language attained in what approximates a five-course program, each course carrying five hours and obtaining five credits. Placement examinations are given a new student entering the college to determine at what level he will begin in the college program. In case a student does better than the established norm of the university for a specific course, he is allowed graduation credit for the course or courses as the case may be and begins in the next higher class.

The department does not claim to have found a panacea for all the language problems, nor does it believe that the present program is final. The program is an evolving and continuing experiment.

DRAMATIZING EVERYDAY EXPERIENCES

At Institution G, students may elect the conversational or the traditional type of course since, within limitations, both types are concurrent. The traditional type of class far outnumbers, of course, the experimental or the conversational.

The classes of the conversational type in French, Spanish, and German are scheduled with respect to contact hours on the same basis—seven hours per week, for the first year, with an additional hour per week spent in lectures on "The Nature of Language," and eight hours for the second year. In each of these three languages, text material adapted to the oral-aural aim is being used. Some of this material is being prepared as the class proceeds, and an effort is made to experiment with the lessons so planned in order to improve the textual material from the teaching standpoint before it is submitted in final form for publication.

An extremely interesting experiment is under way in the elementary intensive French class where an attempt is made to teach French by use of short scenes in dramatized form representing common everyday experiences. The scenes, or playlets, are so arranged as to present a sense of continuity rather than a battery of isolated, non-integrated sets of events. This sense of continuity has a decided value in such a course because of its nature. When the same characters remain throughout the scenes and only the circumstances change, the students are enabled to pass from one scene to the next with no apparent difficulty.

The students meet together three hours a week as a group and perform one of the scenes which they have learned by rote. (Each scene requires two weeks to complete.) Every two weeks a new scene is introduced by the staff members in charge of the course. This new playlet, prepared by a member of the department, is learned by the various staff members who enact it with movements and actions as on a regular stage. (A small stage has been erected for the purpose.) The students are given mimeographed copies of the playlet. Here a transcription in symbols especially devised for the course appears in one column, and in another column the English equivalent in colloquial form is given. No traditional French spelling is presented to the students until late in the second year. No writing is done by the students up to this point. However, it is contemplated that at some point toward the end of the first year both of these elements will be presented, as it is believed something may be lost over the summer vacation unless this is done.

There is an experienced teacher in speech and dramatics who assists the French department during these three hours spent on play acting. When a new scene is to be enacted by the staff members, the dramatics teacher gives the class a brief summary of the scene in English and explains the various actions and intonations involved in it. Then, after the mimeographed papers are handed out to the students, they see two or three repetitions of the scene. Each scene enacted at normal conversational speed requires four or five minutes to perform. The students then write the stage directions into their scripts as dictated by the dramatics teacher. After folding their papers over so that only the French symbols are visible, a member of the staff reads the play in French, sometimes twice if time permits, so that the class becomes familiar with the sounds in relation to the symbols they have before them. This is followed by a further repetition of the performance by the staff. With this the two-hour period is usually over and the students then divide into small groups for practice in learning the parts assigned to them in the remaining four hours of drill. One hour each week, the students have a "walk-through" demonstration with the dramatics teacher in preparation for their "full-dress" performance of the scene on the scheduled day.

The students are apparently able to remember more than one scene at a time, in addition to learning the newly assigned one. The day the class was observed there were four scenes enacted, one of which they had had months before. The pronunciation was good, and the intonation fair. Judging from the movements, actions, and facial expressions, there was excellent comprehension on the part of the class, too. When questioned as to why this particular program was inaugurated, the teacher in charge said that he wanted the students to benefit by the effects of the mimicry-method technique and thus avoid the monotony and tediousness of endless repetitions on the same material with but slight variations from day to day.

There is no basis yet for determining the students' attainments in this class, because it has not gone on for a long enough time to have proven beneficial. In an experiment of this kind, the department feels that at least two years will be required before anything like objective data can be available. Even then the data presented will be on an extremely small scale. The class is purely experimental and must be accepted as such. Certainly appearances, unless they are misleading, seem to indicate that some success is being achieved. If this apparent success continues and has carry-over value, the course will have merit in and by itself.

In Spanish, there are again both conventional and conversational courses with the same contact hours as for French, though the program is not so spectacular. The teachers who assist in this program are shifted every other week so that the students become accustomed to hearing different types of voices and different intonations. The classes for instruction are limited to, twenty-five students and the drill sessions are limited to ten. Reading and writing as well as oral expression and aural comprehension are stressed at the same time, so that the transfer from the first year to the second year will not be too difficult. The second-year program is also largely oral in content and is planned to accommodate those students who have pursued the first-year conversational course.

Various devices are used to make the oral approach successful. In one class, the students began by reading rapidly in Spanish with a fairly good pronunciation. This was followed by discussions in Spanish on elementary, secondary, and university education in Latin America and the United States. Two students were to discuss elementary education, another two, secondary education, and a third group of students, university education. In another class, two students had to discuss the illness of a third party, using the vocabulary they knew pertaining to such a situation. Another group made an introduction of a third party to one another. All the work is done in Spanish and, for the most part, native-born teachers are used.

With respect to the German intensive courses which are styled "semi-intensive" courses, the program is set up to satisfy the two-year language requirements of a reading and speaking knowledge of the language. Material for this two-year course is being prepared by staff members, and in final form it will represent a text or series of texts adapted to a two-year program. The text will be directed to the oral approach and will contain reading material and grammar, but there will also be material to acquaint the student with the background of the people who use it.

The German department felt that the adoption *in toto* of the general organization of the Army course was impossible because of its limited aim. The ultimate aim of the revised foreign language instruction at the university is the attainment of a reading knowledge. The semi-intensive courses in German were established to include development of the aural-oral skills, which was the most striking feature of the Army program. It is believed by the department that, if the students are enabled to express themselves simply in a foreign language within a few weeks, they have already been given an excellent motivation for the study of the language. Therefore, the department adopted a threefold purpose for its two-year program: (1) attainment of a reading knowledge to enable the student to use German effectively in his contact with various fields of learning, (2) acquirement of a fair degree of facility in comprehension and expression of the spoken word, and (3) integration of knowledge of the language with a knowledge of the people, their background and culture.

The first year there are seven contact hours per week of which two are used as analysis periods and five as practice periods. For the second year the course has eight contact hours, four being used as analysis periods and four as practice periods. The analysis periods are devoted to explanation of grammatical problems and presentation of new material, while the practice periods represent drill on the assignments treated in the analysis classes. Analysis sections are limited to twenty-five students and practice periods to ten. Because of the increased class hours, only two hours of home preparation are required per week for the first year, and four hours the second year. All instruction is performed by native or bilingual speakers. No special equipment is used except maps, illustrations, and the like. Experience in the Army programs convinced the German department that phonograph recordings are of little value for classroom use if a native speaker is available for the practice sections.

While the oral approach is maintained throughout the two years, reading occupies an important part in the program, becoming more intensive as the student progresses, so that an extensive vocabulary may be acquired in addition to that learned in the conversational practices. Numerous talks dealing with the geography, history, people, music, art, science, philosophy, and literature of the country are given in English throughout the two-year period.

Though no definite and conclusive proof of the value of this course over the traditional type is yet obtainable, the department believes that this revised two-year program has definite advantages over the traditional college course.

THE INTENSIVE METHOD AS A FOUNDATION

Institution H has a fairly extensive program of language instruction patterned after the Army method of intensive study. There are classes in French, German, Italian, and Spanish, modeled after the ASTP language program. These involve not only subdivision of classes for analysis and drill, or mimicry-memorization and "lab" practice, but they also place primary emphasis on use of the oral approach. The courses provide for eight contact hours per week, normally including four hours' oral practice in small groups. For this intensive course the same credit of four hours accrues as for the traditional beginning courses.

In the French and Spanish departments there were so many students who registered for the intensive oral course that many prearranged plans had to be abandoned and new plans set in order almost overnight. For instance, there were plans to have the class and "lab" sections taught by teachers who had

had experience in the military programs. Again, plans had been made to use instructional materials which had previously been prepared before the opening of school. With the unexpected number of students, however, both of these plans were scrapped. The departments had to use a fairly heterogeneous staff and each day's work had to be thought out continually on a day-by-day basis. In Spanish the number of students who registered for the intensive oral classes was so great that within two hours, over two hundred students had subscribed for these classes. In German the situation was much the same.

The basis of the course in French is a series of brief, carefully prepared dialogues in idiomatic French accompanied by a translation in everyday English. These dialogues are constructed with a view to forcing the students to use real French, no matter how simple, from the very first day, and each dialogue is accordingly brief enough to be learned in two hours' concentrated time. With dialogues such as these, the department felt that the students would eventually be able to enact the dialogues once they were comprehended and once they had become familiar. It was agreed by the department that the students should receive a considerable amount of oral-aural practice before being exposed to the traditional French spelling. Consequently, writing is introduced after two weeks, apparently with good results. Two dictations per week are given throughout the year in addition to the regular examinations and quizzes. However, nothing is ever required of the students in writing unless it can be immediately checked and corrected for their benefit.

It was further agreed by the staff members that no vocabulary items, no idioms, no irregular verbs, and no grammatical principles would be introduced into the course unless they fitted easily and naturally into the dialogues. Therefore, grammar and vocabulary were to be taught from actual French usage. Only complete sentences are used and the new vocabulary is introduced in this way. Grammar is taught functionally, that is, by actual use in a sentence related to the situation to be mastered. Some formal grammar is taught, as must of necessity be done in any class, but no grammatical principle is explained to the student unless he has already had several examples of its use in conversational situations.

Formal reading—so called in this case to differentiate between reading as an assignment and reading traditional French, which the students do from the very first lesson—is introduced in the sixth week. All the usual devices are used: silent reading, paraphrasing, translation, questions and answers in French as to the meaning of a word or idiom in a given passage, and questions to recall similar phrases from the lessons in dialogue form.

The objective of the French classes is not to teach students to speak French instead of teaching them to read it; rather it is to use the intensive method to lay a solid foundation for a later mastery of the language and a thorough understanding of the literature and civilization of France. All four skills are developed in the year of intensive work. Here is a case in which the important question is, how the civilian program can be adapted to the intensive method rather than a question of adapting the intensive method to civilian instruction.

For Spanish a similar but more detailed program of class instruction prevails, with oral expression as the major objective. The classes meet eight hours per week for which four hours of credit is given. However, the division of time, at least for the initial stages, is as follows: mimicry-memorization, three hours; interpretation and analysis, one hour; grammatical practice, one hour; and oral practice, three hours. This distribution of class hours allows for at least six hours of oral practice, if not more, since some oral work will be done in the other two hours of class contact time. It may be well to define briefly what the department means by these terms.

The activity of mimicry-memorization is exactly what its name indicates, imitation of the teacher's pronunciation and rote memory. During the early stages, the students see no Spanish and so they must articulate the sounds without benefit of Spanish orthography. The students repeat ten to twenty times the same expression either individually or in chorus, imitating the teacher until a perfect pronunciation is attained. No approximations are accepted. The interpretation and analysis hour is devoted to explaining any grammatical points contained in the lessons for the week, which students have not clearly understood. The grammatical situations are explained by the presentation of a series of practical exercises in complete sentence form so that the student will learn grammar functionally for the most part.

The weekly hour devoted to grammatical practice is given over to composition work and in this hour some English is used, as there are cases where a given grammatical point cannot be learned by drill and an English sentence must actually be translated into Spanish to satisfy the condition. Composition work is not easily done in an oral class, but all the features of composition writing, grammar, spelling, and syntax can be handled in this hour even when the grammatical point is explained in English. As a rule, the student is not to use English as a means to learn Spanish, except in this grammatical practice hour. The three hours devoted to oral practice are used to fix firmly in the student's mind the text previously studied, only after the teacher is assured that the text of the lesson has already been covered from the standpoint of pronunciation, intonation, and vocabulary in the mimicry-memorization class. For this practice, various approaches are used: questions and answers, dramatizations, completion exercises, given opposites, given synonyms, comprehension games, exchange of personal questions, anecdotes, dialogues, descriptions of students, and so on, all carefully employed and in consonance with the various stages of learning. No matter what devices are used in these oral practice hours, the teacher must keep within the subject matter of the assignments. No new material can be presented unless there is a lag, and then only slight deviations from the schedule are permitted.

From the foregoing, it can be seen that oral work comprises the major emphasis in the elementary intensive Spanish classes and that what the student normally used to do at home, if he studied at all, is now done in the interpretation and analysis class, the grammatical practice class, and the oral practice classes. With so much emphasis on oral work, the department believes it recognizes three successive stages as they evolve in the learning processes: (1) creation of a desire to express thought orally,

(2) spontaneity of expression, and (3) accuracy of expression.

A class in Spanish drill or oral practice calls for some degree of ingenuity and resourcefulness on the part of the teacher, especially if all the approaches mentioned above are brought into play. All classes in Spanish are carefully supervised and controlled by the staff member in charge.

A rather interesting procedure is in operation here which seems to be a necessity if large numbers of students are involved in intensive oral classes. The instructors in charge of these classes form a separate group and meet frequently to discuss the progress made and the difficulties encountered. At these informal staff meetings any new device or technique that seems to have worked out well for the teacher is explained and thus passed on to others. In this way these informal meetings become themselves a kind of teacher-training laboratory. This practice on the part of the department has become a regular weekly matter, and a great deal of discussion is brought out with respect to teaching and teaching problems in the intensive oral classes. What was in the beginning a heterogeneous group of staff members has become as a result of these experiences a closely knit, homogeneous group, so that by consulting a chart, the instructor in charge of all the intensive classes will know exactly what is going on in every class every hour.

For German, which has a much smaller number of students in the intensive oral classes, the procedure and class hours run along the same pattern with some variations. Classes of the traditional and conversational type run parallel with each other and are entirely independent of one another, being under different faculty supervision. Entering students, as is the case for the other language departments, choose between the conversational course which is announced for eight hours per week with relatively little outside preparation and the traditional course which is scheduled for four weekly meetings with the usual amount of homework preparation. Both courses receive four credit hours. The aim of the conversational course is still the reading-ability objective, augmented and reinforced by the active command of spoken words, phrases, and sentences. It is the plan of the department to channel the students of both the conversational and the conventional courses into the same third-semester reading course.

The classes are assigned to one "class or demonstration" section (mimicry-memory and grammatical analysis) and one "laboratory" section (drill), each of which meets four hours a week. In the demonstration classes, students are introduced to simple and useful conversational phrases in German repeated chorally and individually as spoken by the teacher. No reference is made to German spelling or the Fractur type during the first two weeks, when it is assumed that the acoustic pattern of phrases and sentences has been firmly fixed by committing it to memory. In the smaller laboratory classes, the same material is thoroughly reviewed. Grammatical questions, as they present themselves, are treated during the demonstration hours and, if the material warrants it, practiced in oral grammatical drills during the laboratory hours. The frequent repetition of certain pattern phrases and their variations, rather than deduction explanations of grammatical rules and principles, helps to establish a kind of minimum knowledge of grammar which enables the student to continue toward the goal of aural comprehension and command of the spoken language. At the beginning of the third week, a text is introduced, directed to the oral approach.

During the latter part of the first semester, particular attention is accorded to the problem of conversational versus narrative past so that the transfer from an essentially oral type of class to one essentially of the reading type will be more easily made. This transfer, though not impossible, is not easily accomplished because of the different vocabulary encountered in each case and the different grammatical structure. To aid in bridging this gap, the text chosen provides a number of passages in narrative style in which the action of preceding dialogues is condensed and changed into narrative accounts. In the second semester, as it is planned to channel the students of these conversational courses into the same third semester reading course, the students are exposed to some reading identical to that used in the traditional second semester German class. It is apparent that the conversational classes could not complete as much reading material as the traditional classes because of the nature of the approach, but these classes can cover about half the amount prescribed for the traditional classes under proper guidance.

VIII. IMPLEMENTATION AT THE SECONDARY LEVEL

THE QUESTION has often been raised as to whether or not the educational features of the wartime language programs are adaptable to the secondary level. Opinions differ widely with respect to this problem. They range all the way from the view that the secondary school cannot adopt these features to acceptance of practically complete adoption of them all. In the belief that certain of these features were applicable to, and even desirable for, the lower schools, the Commission on Implications authorized the establishment of an experimental program on the secondary level.[1]

It was decided that, if the experiment was to be undertaken, it should concern more than one language and, since time was an important item, that the entire experiment be conducted in the same institution. For these reasons, one of the large high schools in New York City was finally chosen.

Although the suggestion of an experiment was enthusiastically received and full cooperation was promised by all the individuals concerned, it was pointed out that the new term would begin within two days and that the utmost haste was necessary. Actually no time was left to make elaborate plans, to work out in detail a course of study, or even to make a scientific selection of pupils.

Classes were organized in French, German, and Spanish, since there happened to be two beginners' classes in each language. Three classes were simply designated as "experimental" classes and three as "control" classes. There was no time to group the pupils on the basis of intelligence or prognostic tests; the bet-

---

[1] Adapted from a report on the experiment by Dr. Theodore Huebener, director of foreign languages, New York City public schools. For other programs on this level, see William G. Meyer, "Nutley High School's Plan of Language Teaching," *German Quarterly*, XVIII (November 1945), 172–73; Esther M. Eaton, "Can High School Modern Language Study Pay Dividends?" *Modern Language Journal*, XXX (January 1946), 20–26; Stephen L. Pitcher, "Application of ASTP Experience to Language Teaching in Secondary and Elementary Schools," *Hispania*, XXIX (May 1946), 190–96.

ter class was made the special class and the other the control group.

All six classes met five days a week during the spring term of 1946, that is, from February 6 to June 14.[2] Each of the three special classes was supplied with a set of Kany elementary conversation manuals. The actual oral work in class, however, was largely spontaneous and was developed by the teacher as the occasion demanded. Much of this work, especially in the beginning, consisted of questions and answers. Very soon, though, students were called upon to interrogate classmates, to give orders, to paraphrase, to dramatize, and to give brief descriptions or narrations.

Naturally, constant demands were made on the teachers' resourcefulness and inventiveness. Since they were young, affirmative personalities, they acquitted themselves well. Their sense of humor was especially valuable in lending sparkle and gaiety to prolonged oral activities, which in less skillful hands might have become dull and monotonous.

Emphasis was placed on accuracy in pronunciation, although there was no resort to phonetic transcriptions.

In the absence of scientific measurements and tests, the conclusions arrived at had to be based almost wholly on the teachers' and supervisors' reactions. Even though their opinions lack the force of scientific validity, they are presented in the hope that they may shed some light on the problems involved.

THE STUDENTS

As stated earlier, no time was available for regrouping the already organized classes for the experiment. The composition of the two French classes was distinctly different. In the special class there were forty-one students, thirty of whom were honor-school pupils.[3] In the control class of thirty-eight, six were repeaters and only nineteen were normal beginning students. In other words, the special class was a bright group, the control class a dull one.

---

[2] The experimental classes continued for a second semester to qualify for tests with established national norms.

[3] Honor pupils are those who during the preceding term attained an average of 90 percent or more in all subjects.

Of the thirty-six students in the German class, sixteen had an IQ of 125 or over and twenty were between 94-124. Thirty of them were second-language students. The teacher felt that the class contained a larger number of poor students than is common in first term German classes in this school.

In the Spanish experimental class there were thirteen honor-school students, eleven first-language students, three second-language students, and two repeaters.

PLAN SUGGESTED

With a view to providing something definite by which to be guided, the following set of instructions was issued:

Oral Method in Foreign Languages

The following suggestions are made in an attempt to specify more definitely what procedures are to be used in the so-called oral method. This, of course, can be only of a general nature and must be subject to modifications due to local conditions and unforeseen exigencies.

The method is to be tried out in a beginners' class in French, Spanish, and, if possible, German. For each experimental class there is to be a control group taught by the traditional method.

To increase the validity of the experiment the students involved should all be of equal intelligence and ability, as far as possible. There ought to be no wide disparities in intelligence or in reading quotient.

The experiment is to be conducted this coming term, beginning February 4.

For each language an unusually competent teacher should be selected and one who is sincerely interested in the outcome of this experiment.

The experimental classes are to be taught by the oral method, that is, the direct method in which the foreign language is used exclusively from the start.

The classroom work will consist of questions and answers, memorization, paraphrasing, dramatized dialogue, the carrying out of simple commands, the performance of Gouin series, etc.

The teacher may use the board, particularly for illustrative purposes. The pupils, however, will not be called upon to write on the board.

There will be no translations from the foreign language into English except to clarify, on rare occasions, a word or phrase.

Much attention will be devoted to correct pronunciation, phrasing, and intonation. The speech pattern will be of pre-eminent importance.

Some reading may be done in the classroom. Brief selections on which conversation can be based are particularly suitable for this purpose.

The course will involve home preparation. This preparation will be of the nature of reading, oral practice, and memorization. The pupil will not be required to do written exercises.

Another important feature of the work will be practice in comprehension. The teacher will read or present orally brief passages or stories to which students will listen and then answer questions orally. The reading matter can also be reworked for oral practice.

The grammar is to be functional. Type sentences will prove useful.

Possibly, in the explanation of more involved points of grammar, resort will have to be had to English. This, however, should be done as little as possible.

Right from the start, vocabulary and idioms should be built up around themes increasing in difficulty and complexity.

Since there is no adequate textbook on the market, it will undoubtedly be necessary to prepare mimeographed material.

As outcomes of the course, we may expect the acquisition of possibly 300 words of active vocabulary, 30 active idioms and an equal number of passive words and idioms recognized visually and aurally.

Tests on the pupils' ability should be entirely oral, in order to test their ability to comprehend, to reply to questions, to carry out commands, to engage in a simple dialogue, and to develop a simple theme orally.

Because several contingencies could not be foreseen, the above plan had to be modified extensively. Again because of the haste with which the experiment was organized, it was impossible to work out a course in detail, and each of the three teachers had to be left to his own devices. Naturally, there were some divergences. These will be pointed out below under the consideration of each phase of the work.

For brevity and easy recognition, the three teachers will be designated by the initials of their respective languages, i.e., F, G, and S.

OBJECTIVES AND MATERIALS

Aim

The teachers were told that they were to use the foreign language exclusively and that their objective was to teach the pupil to speak. This aim was followed with some modifications. Teacher F stated as her aim, "To develop the ability to comprehend both written and spoken French, and to converse in French." Teacher G, appreciating the fact that what was being done had to be accomplished within a given framework by pupils who were going on into regular classes, stated as his objective, "The aim has been to develop maximum proficiency in spoken German, while at the same time fulfilling the various requirements of the city and departmental syllabi for the language." Teacher S merely set out "To develop as much conversational ability as possible." All three teachers believe they attained their aim, although G qualified it by adding, "But not to the extent hoped for."

Materials

With any group, but especially with beginners, the teacher cannot be expected to go very far without some printed text to follow or something on which to base conversation at least. One could, of course, imagine a resourceful teacher who would plan and mimeograph conversation units or exercises for each lesson. It would have been unreasonable to demand this additional amount of work from teachers handling five classes daily with a pupil load around 200. Furthermore, it was precluded by the lack of time in setting up the experiment.

All three classes were provided with copies of the corresponding Kany elementary conversation manual. There were used also: in German, Betz and Price, *A First German Book;* and in Spanish, Wilkins, *Primeros Pasos.*

Since there were no audio-visual materials immediately available, none were used. Teacher G employed maps for reference.

PROCEDURES
Method

The method followed in these classes was primarily a form of the approach known as "direct." However, it was a modified rather than a purely direct method. The essential traits of the traditional direct method are:

1. Thorough training in practical phonetics.
2. Grammatical rules limited to those "which are important, frequent, and regular."

3. Grammar taught from the language itself rather than by abstract principles.

4. Speaking, the most significant feature of the direct method, taught in combination with hearing, reading, and writing.

5. Translation resorted to as little as possible.

6. The dramatized series of Gouin used to act out sentences and commands.

7. Materials selected with the aim of acquainting the student with the foreign culture.

In class, the above features of the direct method could only be realized in part, chiefly because these were first-term classes.

Although accuracy in pronunciation was stressed, one could not very well speak of "a thorough training in phonetics." The same was true of the grammar. No attempt was made to formulate rules; all grammar points were taught by extensive practice with examples. Translation was not used at all.

No materials were available "to acquaint the student with the foreign culture." Furthermore, the opportunity to use such materials would not arise until much later, after a firm hold had been acquired on fundamental principles and basic grammar.

Typical lesson

Each teacher was more or less left to work out his own lesson procedures to achieve the aim designated.

In French the order was:

1. A new selection was read by the teacher and repeated, sentence by sentence, by the class.

2. Questions were given on the text and answered in French and English.

3. For stories prepared at home, pupils were required to give oral summaries and to answer questions in French.

4. For practice in conversation, pupils were asked to talk freely on a given topic in the manual. New words, required by the pupils, were given them by the teacher.

5. Each period usually ended with the singing of a song or the recitation of a poem.

In German the plan followed was: (1) assignment for next day placed on board, (2) exchange of greetings and conversation practice, (3) going over the oral and written homework, (4) presentation of new grammar points, (5) conversation, and (6) samples of written or oral homework drilled.

In Spanish, the teacher put new words and expressions on the board for the class. After these were studied and drilled, they were used, under the teacher's guidance, to develop a given topic.

Use of foreign language and of English

The foreign language was used almost exclusively in each of the classes. New points in grammar, however, were explained in English. Also, English was resorted to whenever necessary for comprehension.

Preparation and note-taking

Teachers G and S assigned homework regularly. Teacher S assigned exercises from the text, Spink and Millis, and also had the pupils memorize short conversations from the Kany manual. In French and German the students took notes on vocabulary and grammar. Teacher G frequently dictated. Teacher S gave no notes.

PHASES OF INSTRUCTION

Reading

The proportion of time given to reading was as follows:

In French about two-fifths of the time was given to reading.

In German about ten minutes daily were devoted to the reading of textbook selections and five minutes to reading from the board.

In Spanish one-fifth of the time was devoted to reading. The basic books were used essentially:

1. To cover the grammatical points required of first-term students, and
2. As a basis for conversation.

The Kany conversation booklets were used as:

1. Models for conversations.
2. Models for copying.
3. Sources of material for memorization.

In all three languages some reading was done; it was done most consistently in the French class. The daily selection formed the basis of the oral drills, conversation, and written answers. As an occasional test, the teacher would present a totally new selection to the class.

The progress in reading appeared to be satisfactory. Teacher G comments: "The reading is generally good, shows comprehension, and is intelligently modulated, phrased, and intoned."

Grammar

The points in grammar required by the New York (City) Syllabus of Minima in Foreign Languages are as follows:

French

Articles: definite and indefinite; singular and plural; contraction of definite article with *à* and *de*.
Nouns: regular formation of plural.
Adjectives: agreement and position of regular adjectives; possessives; cardinal numerals one–sixty-nine.
Pronouns: personal, used as subject.
Verbs: present indicative of the first conjugation, and of *avoir* and *être*. Negative, *ne. . . pas.*
Preposition: *de* to indicate possession.
Interrogation.

German

Articles: definite and indefinite, and *der* and *ein* words. (Of the *der* words, only *dieser, jeder, jenner,* and *welcher* to be emphasized.)
Nouns: the singular and plural in all cases. But the classification into declension groups is unnecessary, plurals being learned as vocabulary. Rules to be reduced to the three helpful ones, namely: (1) feminine polysyllables add *-n* or *-en*; (2) nearly all nouns with the singular ending *-e* add *-n*; (3) *-chen* and *-lein* remain unchanged.

A list of forty high frequency nouns to be selected from the basic book in use should be memorized with their "principal parts." These are to be made a part of the pupils' active vocabulary, so that they may be used with a high degree of accuracy. They will supply a foundation on which to build in subsequent terms.

Pronouns: personal, third person, nominative, dative, and accusative, singular and plural; no genitives; first and second persons, nominative, singular and plural; other cases as vocabulary only. Interrogatives, *wer* and *was*. Combinations such as *womit, wovon,* etc., to be learned as vocabulary.

Verbs: present indicative of weak verbs and of strong verbs without irregularities; of *haben* and *sein;* of a few very common strong verbs with irregularities, such as *sehen, lesen, sprechen, nehmen, fahren, fallen, halten.* The regular imperative and the imperative of *sein, nehmen, sehen,* and *lesen.*

Prepositions: the nine "doubtfuls" (*an, auf,* etc.) for thorough and accurate use. The commoner dative and accusative prepositions such as *mit, von, zu, durch,* and *für,* as vocabulary.

Word order: normal and inverted.

Conjunctions: coordinating only, and these restricted to *und, aber, oder, denn.*

Spanish

Articles: definite and indefinite; *al* and *del.*

Nouns: gender; number; possession.

Adjectives: gender; number; agreement; possessives; cardinal numerals 1—1,000,000.

Pronouns: personal, used as subject and as direct object; one object with the finite verb; prepositional forms.

Verbs: present indicative of regular verbs, and of *ser, estar,* and *tener; ser* with predicate complement; *estar* to denote position.

All three teachers taught at least as much grammar as is given in the regular class. The amount acquired, however, seemed to vary.

(F) Somewhat more grammar was acquired.

(G) All of the grammar for the first term was presented. It was acquired "to a slightly lesser degree than is generally the case."

(S) More grammar was learned.

Writing

The amount of time devoted to writing varied somewhat in the three classes.

(F) About one-fifth of the time was given to writing.

(G) About ten minutes daily were given over to writing the homework on the board and correcting it.

(S) About one-fifth of each period was devoted to writing.

Vocabulary

A considerably larger amount of vocabulary was acquired. Teacher G said that it was twenty percent more; teacher S said that it ran as high as 500 words.

Pronunciation

Although practically no attention was given to systematic instruction in phonetics and no phonetic transcriptions were taught, the quality of the pronunciation achieved by the students was rather good in all classes.

CONVERSATION

General comments

In a first-term class, conversation—the free spontaneous exchange of ideas in the foreign language—can hardly be spoken of. More correctly one can speak only of oral activities based on a limited vocabulary and a very elementary grammatical framework.

Unconsciously, the speaking had to be linked up with the "reading aim," proving again the close interrelationship between various phases of language activities. In the beginning the oral work is primarily vocalizing difficult sounds and sound groups. It is the preparatory step to speaking. With reference to the latter, distinction must be made between controlled speaking and imitative speaking. Reproducing passages from memory is imitative speaking. Free speaking cannot be attempted to any great extent until much later.

How practised

Most of the oral work was based on the reading in French and German. In Spanish, the teacher gave to the class new words and expressions to be used in talking about a given topic, or rather, forming simple sentences.

TESTING DEVICES

Daily tests

Brief oral and written tests were given to determine the progress of the students.

Final test

It was originally planned to test each special class together with the control group in oral facility. This had to be abandoned because the scheduling of classes, affecting the entire student body, allowed no free time for this purpose.

At the close of the term in June, the special class and the control class were given the same final examination. This examination was of the regular type, testing primarily reading and grammar attainment.

RESULTS IN FINAL EXAMINATIONS

	FRENCH		GERMAN		SPANISH	
Percentage	Special	Control	Special	Control	Special	Control
Below 55......	0	11	0	4	5	2
55–64.........	0	2	1	3	3	3
65–74.........	3	5	2	5	7	6
75–84.........	6	4	3	10	8	4
85–94.........	18	14	5	15	6	5
95–100........	14*	1	25	1	1	1
	41	37	36	38	30	21

* Of the 14 students getting between 95 and 100 in the special class, 7 attained 100 percent or perfect papers. This, of course, is not strange when one considers that 30 of these students were honor-school pupils.

It will be seen from the above tabulation that the experimental classes in French and German did considerably better than the control classes. On the other hand, the special class in Spanish did not perform materially better. It did, however, perform about as well as the control class. It should be added that the special class in Spanish was considerably larger than the control class.

REACTIONS

Of supervisors

A number of observations of these classes were made by the principal, a member of the Commission Staff, the two chairmen, and the Director of Foreign Languages for New York City. On each occasion they were rather favorably impressed with what they saw and heard. The spirit of the class was good and the pupils were apparently learning to speak with confidence and a commendable degree of accuracy.

Of students

In all three classes the teachers reported eagerness on the part of the pupils to recite. "They seem to enjoy this type of instruction. Some have told me they like the fact that they are learning to converse in French."

Of the teachers

Since the teachers were the ones to work out and conduct the experiment, their views are without question the most valuable. Some of their reactions are given below.

The teacher of the French class says:

I enjoyed working with this special class. I felt that the students have accomplished more in this class than they would in a regular class. They have gained a greater knowledge of French, have learned to express themselves orally to a larger degree and to comprehend better both written and spoken French. I believe that in such a class the students have a greater feeling of achievement and self-confidence at the end of the term than in the ordinary regular class. However, I don't believe such a course should be given to any other than students of higher than average intelligence or second-language students. I don't think it would be successful for ordinary pupils. The class size should be definitely limited to from thirty to thirty-five pupils to allow for greater individual work.

The teacher of the German class comments as follows:

Conversation adds a good facet of interest to the course if it can be made natural or real. It also supplied a good apperceptive mass and motivation for other phases of class work.

Perforce, the conversation situation is generally stilted, unnatural, painfully repetitious, and exhausting to the teacher.

In a course which aims to fulfil the requirements of a "normal" class, this method proves an obstacle because of time consumed by learning conversation patterns and drilling at the expense of other required and necessary phases of instruction.

Given the normal class as the constant, or the norm, this class falls slightly below the level of an average class in all phases of work, except pronunciation, reading, and *prepared* conversation.

This teacher, in the course of the term, has gradually arrived at the firm conviction that this method cannot form the core of the two-year high school course in German as now constituted.

It is his belief that the method has very great intrinsic value indeed, but that it cannot be given its due in a high school. For example, the class here discussed had to content itself with covering fewer lessons in grammar than those required of Term 1, and it had to forego studying the required portion of the cultural syllabus entirely. It is open to question whether the class will be able to make up this deficiency before the Regents' examination.

This type of course, in the opinion of this teacher, belongs in the seventh and eighth years of the elementary school. In the high school, classes are too large for this type of work in terms of the amount of time available. . . . If this course were to be tried on the elementary school level (or on a laboratory basis in the high school *in addition* to regular class work), then it would pay very high dividends.

As it was, the extreme dependence on models and the continual need for correction inhibited free speech and caused a loss of inventiveness. In order to avoid a concatenation of oral inaccuracies, the teacher was forced to prompt continually. Without proper grounding, conversation in the beginning is too imitative and too groping to prove either effective or enjoyable.

The Spanish teacher says:

Conversation as an objective in language teaching is highly desirable. In fact, reading should furnish merely the subject-matter for speaking. If the pupil acquires oral competence, he will also read with ease.

However, none of the phases of a language should be neglected, since they are all closely connected. One cannot learn a language without listening, speaking, reading, and writing.

There must be writing and spelling at the beginning as well as speaking. Printed translations should accompany the text. Model conversational patterns should be provided. For the sake of economy, all grammatical points should be explained in English. If the pupils are drilled sufficiently on essential vocabularies, they will be able to employ them in free, spontaneous, oral composition which is the basis of conversation.

CONCLUSIONS

1. With a resourceful, dynamic teacher, the intensive oral method can be used successfully even in beginners' classes on the secondary level.

2. However, unrelieved oral activities may prove burdensome to the teacher and monotonous to the pupil.

3. In view of the interrelation of the various phases of language, writing and reading cannot afford to be neglected.

4. Reading particularly proves most useful in providing the basis for oral activities and conversation.

5. To attain its maximum effectiveness, special reading materials and conversation models must be supplied. The ordinary language textbook is not adequate.

6. Oral activities in the beginning are severely limited by lack

of vocabulary and grammatical knowledge on the part of the pupil. True conversation cannot be engaged in until later.

7. Language facts must be learned and drilled. Then they can be used in conversation. This would point to the "laboratory" period which has been successfully used in some schools in the third year.

8. A purely oral approach would seem to be more natural with younger children, in the seventh and eighth grades.

9. The intensive oral method would be the most effective one to use in advanced grades in high school or in a specialized high school where a practical command of the language for vocational ends is the objective.

10. In the high school as now constituted, *conversation* cannot be accepted as a reasonable objective in foreign language instruction. For the large majority of students the foreign language is only another school subject. Their main interest may lie elsewhere and only a very small portion of them will ever put a language to practical use in travel, research, or correspondence. For them the broader cultural and educational values must remain paramount.

11. As far as the immediate objective is concerned, the aim of foreign-language teaching should be to equip the student, through daily practice in reading, writing, and speaking, with the absolutely necessary fundamentals of the language, so that he has a firm foundation on which to build if he is to make practical use of the language later in life.

12. If the intensive oral method of the armed forces is to be used with equal effectiveness in the schools, equally favorable conditions must be provided. Essentially these are more time, smaller classes, laboratory periods, adequate materials, highly selected students, and motivation based solely on the utility of the subject. Since, however, the aim of the school must be basically cultural, and since the expensiveness of the intensive method of instruction would be totally unjustifiable in the case of the average student, this method would be the one to use only where the aim is utilitarian. That would be in a specialized high school with linguistically gifted students seeking to attain skill mastery for vocational competence.

IX. THE UNIVERSITY OF CHICAGO LANGUAGE INVESTIGATION

A NUMBER of experiments have been carried on in the past few years relating to the teaching of foreign languages. These experiments have concerned not only Americans of English speech who are learning a second language, but also Americans of foreign extraction and some of our Latin-American neighbors who desire to learn English as their second language. The most comprehensive program yet undertaken in this experimental field was the foreign area and language curriculum of the Army Specialized Training Program. Opinions on the value of these programs up to the present have been largely subjective. There is no objective evidence relating to the experimental programs which supports or denies existing judgments.

In order to determine both immediate and future values of these experimental ventures, the Rockefeller Foundation believed that a careful and impartial investigation of language teaching should be made. For this purpose, the Foundation established a project at the University of Chicago, entitled "The Investigation of the Teaching of a Second Language," under the direction of Ralph W. Tyler.

This project is attempting to evaluate current experimental teaching of modern foreign languages in the schools and colleges of the country, largely in the so-called "intensive" courses patterned after the foreign-language curriculum of the ASTP. One of the major phases of this educational project is to develop a testing program for measuring types and levels of skill allegedly imparted through intensive instruction, and to compare the results with those attained in the traditional courses.

TESTING PROGRAM

To measure adequately the worth of intensive versus traditional instruction, a battery of tests covering the aural, oral, and reading skills in both types of course must be available. Standardized tests already exist with established national norms for the testing of reading. For the measurement of aural comprehension and oral facility, the investigating staff has had to prepare new types of tests. It was hoped that by administering these to a large number of students on different levels national norms for oral production and aural comprehension could be established.

For the testing of reading the investigation is availing itself of the tests of the Cooperative Test Service. These are standardized instruments with an established national reputation. For measuring the aural and oral skills, however, the investigation has constructed and administered its own battery of tests. This has been done for French, German, Russian, and Spanish.

For testing aural comprehension, the testing material, spoken by carefully selected native speakers, was recorded on phonograph records. As the student listens to the record, he has before him a test-booklet and a specially designed answer-sheet for machine-scoring. Each test consists of three parts, requires a maximum of fifty minutes, and may be given to any number of students at a time.

The lower level tests are designed for students with a running total of 90 to 130 class hours. Part One consists of twenty-five completion items, each with a triple-choice response (worded in English) ; Part Two consists of twenty-five definition items, each with a triple-choice response; Part Three is made up of six short anecdotes, with from five to nine triple-choice responses, worded in English, on the content of each.

The make-up of the French Lower Level Test differs from that of the other languages in that the Completion Series is replaced by thirty Phonetic Accuracy items, each with a quadruple-choice response.

The upper level tests are intended for students having a running total of more than 150 class hours. Part One consists of twenty-five definitions; Part Two is composed of six anecdotes with from six to nine triple-choice responses on each; Part Three consists of a five-minute dialogue between a man and a woman, with fifteen triple-choice responses on its content.

For testing oral production, individual tests have been compiled on two levels, and feature (1) oral response to pictorial stimuli, and (2) controlled conversation with a native speaker through the use of phonograph records.[1]

The data which follow have been drawn from a memorandum furnished by Professor Agard of the investigating staff.

The test administration was widely extended, particularly the aural comprehension which was given between April 1945 and July 1946, in 45 colleges and 37 secondary schools. Thanks to a wide response by teachers and administrators, the groups tested included not only students in the experimental intensive courses at centers where programs of cooperation with the investigators were arranged, but also many hundreds of students following language courses of the conventional type. As a special feature of the undertaking, a considerable proportion of the students were retested for progress after an interval of three or more months, with the use of the same or alternative test forms. As an index of this broad sampling, it is worth noting that the French aural tests were administered at the lower level to 1,515 students in colleges and 273 in secondary schools; at the upper level, to 1,115 and 169 respectively. In Spanish, the figures ran to 2,149 and 1,549 in the colleges, and 1,521 and 883 in the secondary schools.

Since the question of attainment in the several skills in the intensive and conventional courses is of vital interest, the investigation tested both groups at comparable stages of achievement. While the number of colleges was not large where this type of control could be applied, it is nevertheless to be hoped that some light will be thrown on the relative achievement in the various language skills by the intensive method and the conventional procedure.

Thus far (August 1946), norms have been established only on the scores of students in conventional courses. When separate norms are set up for those examined in the intensive courses, the stage will be set for a study of significant differences in achievement.

The oral production tests were administered by a local administrant according to a carefully prepared rating of 2, 1, and

---

[1] Adapted from the detailed description of tests in *Modern Language Journal,* XXIX (November 1945), 633–34.

0 points per utterance. The administration of these was not so broad as in the case of the aural tests; and the experimental administrations of the oral will have to be followed by standardization, which will presuppose administration with the aid of individual recording and objective scoring of the responses by a central examining authority.

Concurrently with oral and aural achievement, the investigation has also measured broadly achievement in reading, vocabulary, and grammar for French, German, and Spanish classes by the use of testing instruments of the Cooperative Test Service.

OTHER AIMS OF THE INVESTIGATION

Since the intensive course proposes as a primary objective the ability to speak the foreign language as well as to understand it when spoken, and at the same time adheres to the acquisition of reading ability as a final goal, the investigation should go far to clarify a number of issues. Some of the problems which it hopes to try to solve concern the degree to which the proposed objectives are attained, whether or not equally good results will accrue for the average college students as were claimed for the specially selected and highly motivated Army personnel. Another real problem which the investigation may help to solve concerns the greater number of hours and the smaller classes which were characteristic of the ASTP language curriculum. Are these justifiable and practicable in civilian education? If the investigation can show that students gain greater proficiency through these procedures, then undoubtedly more educational institutions will be willing to make the necessary adjustments.

The investigation will terminate at the end of the year 1947, when findings will be published for general distribution.

X. AREA-STUDY PROGRAMS IN CIVILIAN INSTITUTIONS

AREA STUDY, like the intensive language classes, is being widely considered for adoption in various institutions, but very few programs are in actual operation. Plans are under way, however, to establish areal programs in civilian institutions with varying degrees of integration. Some of the programs in operation may be prewar creations which have received some influence, either direct or indirect, by the presence of the war-time area program. There are, however, a few programs which owe their existence entirely to the wartime experience with them, while others, in existence before the war, have adopted some of their educational features—intensive classes and an attempt at integration. On the other hand, there have been in existence a number of schools of international affairs, and a few colleges have for a long time offered what has been designated as an "interdepartmental major." Area study is something again quite different from either of these, and yet it is in a sense related to them.

A carefully planned areal program attempts to integrate the numerous ideas and the seemingly disparate knowledge about an area so as to present the total picture of that area and the learning of the language plays an important part, since one is placed in a position to see how the people of that area think and act. On the other hand, in the programs of international affairs and of interdepartmental majors, several separate disciplines may be brought into play, but the courses run concurrently or sequentially with no very great concern for integration. If the language is entirely omitted in these programs, or if too many languages are involved as is the case when a large world area is under examination, the practical aspect characteristic of the wartime programs is almost lost.

That many institutions have been making plans for the establishment of areal programs is indicative that such programs proved valuable and sound. Whether civilian institutions will ultimately adopt area studies similar to those established by the Army and Navy will depend on many factors. Are there qualified personnel? Are there competent linguists in the language of the area? Does the institution have adequate library or exhibit facilities relating to the area for which it hopes to establish a course of study? These and many other related questions must be answered before an areal program can be considered for adoption by the institution.

The various armed services and many government agencies borrowed heavily on personnel from civilian institutions to service their needs, so that it was difficult to man properly even the fifty-five foreign area and language programs that existed during the war. Will this personnel return to their respective institutions? Where and how will experienced, or even inexperienced though competent, personnel be found as replacements? Some institutions which would like to plan for an areal program are prevented because suitable personnel are not presently available, even though they may have adequate library and physical facilities. For this reason among others, few programs will be in operation in the immediate future.

Though area study may be planned on a far wider basis than the scope of this study can hope to estimate due to its limitations, there are a few programs worth mentioning for what they are in the face of the above-mentioned difficulties.

Area studies should be of interest on a scale of priorities deriving from their importance in education and in international relations so far as can be predicted. Area studies will be tempered, of course, by the extent to which they are already developed. A possible priorities arrangement might include the following in the order given: the Slavs, the Far East, the Arabic world, the Indic world, Southeastern Asia, Central Asia, Central Africa, and other areas. In this imaginary priorities list, the Latin-American area and the European have been omitted, since they are fields which have for some time claimed interest in this country.[1] The goals ought to be development of ade-

---

[1] Cf. *Notes on Latin-American Studies*, No. 1 (April 1943), Joint Committee on Latin-American Studies. European Area Studies are already somewhat developed, and again the related languages do not present the same obstacles as the Far Eastern.

quate area study in academic institutions at the following levels: general education, vocational minors, areal majors, graduate study and research. Inasmuch as a university cannot be all things to all individuals, it is not likely that any one institution will be able to offer area-study programs for all areas or to think of them on every level. This will allow, and rightly so, for that interplay between the various institutions of higher learning which has been characteristic of higher education in America throughout its diversified history, since it is an accepted cardinal principle that the democratic ideal cannot be fulfilled upon any desirable or significant level without this differentiation of function.[2] From many angles and from many points of view, then, area study may have a very wide and worthwhile future.

AREA-STUDY PROGRAMS IN OPERATION

How well the current planners of area-study programs have taken into account the above-mentioned possibilities as well as the related contingencies may be seen by the following descriptions of courses based on a questionnaire furnished by the American Council of Learned Societies and the published university bulletins. Lack of space allows for mention of but a few. The names of the institutions proposing programs in area studies have not been disclosed due either to the experimental basis on which they are established or to the tentative nature of the various planning stages involved. Though three or four institutions have published bulletins on their programs, it is considered wise to treat all institutions on the same anonymous basis. There are, however, in the enumerations that follow a number of possibilities and suggestive ideas.

Institution A

Through integrated programs of area studies coupled with intensive instruction in the respective language, it will be possible for students at this institution to concentrate in one of the fol-

[2] Cf. Henry M. Wriston, "Differentiation of Function," *North Central Association Quarterly*, IX (October 1935), 144, 145, and 148.

lowing regions: Latin America, Latin Europe, Central Europe, and Eastern Europe. Prerequisites for admission to the field of concentration will be six approved hours in each—history, government, and economics—and a demonstrated linguistic aptitude and an elementary knowledge of one of the languages involved. Concentration will begin normally with the junior year, and each program is to include (a) the Area Core Course which will be a cooperative venture under the direction of a major instructor with special lecturers and consultants collaborating, and will be specially designed to give unity and clarity to the area characteristics; (b) the Area Seminar, where planned research in area topics based on primary sources will enable the individual student to acquire the experience and method of independent study and investigation; (c) an intensive course in one language to be studied eight hours per week, in small groups under both native and American instructors, for two years, or less if the requirement of conversational ability is previously satisfied.

Provision is to be made for the equipment and maintenance of a *realia* room for each of the areas.

The program will have pre-professional and cultural aims on the undergraduate level, and will provide professional training at the graduate level, leading to the degree of master of arts.

Institution B

In order to train men in the field of language and international relations for service with both public and private agencies at a time of greatly increased national need, the committee responsible for setting up the course of study recommends the introduction in 1946–47 of one or two experimental regional programs (probably the Soviet Union and China) to be available both to graduate students and to qualified undergraduates. The undergraduate and graduate regional curricula would be much the same for the first year, but would differ in important respects in the second year. Minimum requirements for undergraduates entering the program would be one basic course in a social science other than history.

Concentration in area study proper would begin about the

junior year, and the pattern of the program would be somewhat like this:

Junior Year (four full courses)

a) One double intensive language course
b) One double integrated regional course

Senior Year

a) One half-course, advanced, in the language
b) Two advanced regional half-courses
c) One half-course in an approved field relevant both to the region and to general education
d) Distinction thesis
e) General examination

The double regional course would meet six times a week during two terms and would present an integrated picture of the region largely from the point of view of the social sciences, but would not neglect the relevant philosophic, artistic, and literary considerations. The double language course would also extend through two semesters, meeting three times a week for formal work in language structure and five times for aural-oral drill and reading. This would be followed by a final half-course (perhaps more in some languages) in the senior year, so that the two courses would attempt to give those students who have demonstrated linguistic ability an effective use of the language. If students were able to take the double language course in the sophomore year, they would be able to make effective use of the language for the regional work that much sooner. The advanced regional courses would follow the basic double regional course with the end in view of presenting more specialized regional problems. Such an advanced course reaching into a number of disciplines would be most effectively given on the same integrated basis as the double regional course.

The graduate curriculum would follow the same general pattern as that on the undergraduate level. The degree would be one of achievement and would require normally two years. The master's thesis and oral examination would play much the same roles as the undergraduate distinction thesis and general examination.

Institution C

Area and language studies are proposed at this university to be of special value to students in various fields, i.e., foreign service of the United States, overseas positions with government civilian agencies, positions with industrial and commercial firms engaged in foreign trade, public health and welfare agencies, journalism, teaching of the social studies, geography, and business, air transportation, and general research. The area and language program is an outgrowth of older plans set up before the war, but was fortified and strengthened by the Army programs. There will be areal programs offered on Latin America, China, and the Far East, Russia, Germany, and France. A typical program for the Latin-American Area is the following:

Geography—Mexico and the Caribbean.
Geography—Geography of northern South America: Venezuela, Colombia, Ecuador, the Guianas, and Brazil.
History—History of Latin America.
Fine Arts—Arts in Spain and her colonies.
Geography—Southern South America: Argentina, Uruguay, Paraguay, Chile, Bolivia, and Peru.
Sociology—Social life and social relations among the peoples of Central and South America.
Language—Portuguese and Spanish, a total of eighteen to twenty-two hours required, with additional courses for advanced students, using the intensive method developed by the ASTP, or such adaptations of it as are suitable at the various levels of language study.

Courses in this program may be counted toward college degrees in the usual manner.

Institution D

Institution D has established a School of International Affairs which is an outgrowth of one of the wartime educational projects which it sponsored. The school should not, however, be considered the direct result of this wartime program. Other departments and schools within the university had for a number of years offered programs in international affairs. The newly created school will place more emphasis on area study and the related languages than was true of the earlier programs which, with the wartime programs it sponsored, are responsible for its existence.

The purpose of the school is to provide a course of instruction which will equip the students for staff and administrative posts in international fields. For this purpose the curriculum has been designed with these objectives in view: to provide the student with a satisfactory factual background in international affairs; to give him, in so far as an academic program can, an understanding of the forces and factors operating in these fields; and to develop his technical competence in a specialty such as international law, economics, business administration, government service, or administration, enabling him to put his general knowledge into practical use. The program will require two years for completion, leading finally to the master's degree.

Basic requirements for admission are: a bachelor's degree or equivalent, a superior undergraduate record, and a better than average performance on the Graduate Record Examination. In addition, the student must satisfy the special requirements of the functional field in which he plans to specialize, such as business affairs, economic affairs, government affairs, international administration, or legal affairs.

The first year's curriculum is divided into three sections. The first section contains courses which are designed to give the student some idea of the political and economic focus in the institutions which have developed in the major countries of the world and to show both their national and international import. The second section contains courses to familiarize the student with political, economic, and social institutions, customs, and traditions of some significant geographic area. The third section contains courses which are designed to give the student facility in the language of the area of primary interest.

For the second year, there are courses arranged in five groups or divisions, each group representing the program of study for the fields of specialization, identical to those listed above. Each of these divisions represents a functional field of concentration from among which the student may choose and in one of which he must specialize. Since the program is somewhat more prescriptive than elective, adjustments may have to be made to avoid duplication of work by students who enter the school with any previous special training. The degree of master of international affairs will be awarded to the student upon satisfactory completion of the program and compliance with the requirements of the university.

For the present, three areas of concentration are offered: Europe, with emphasis upon German culture; Europe, with emphasis upon French culture; and Russia. In addition to the prescribed general and area courses, each student is required to pursue such courses in the language of the area upon which he is concentrating so that he can read and write the language and use it orally with some degree of proficiency.

The Russian program will be undertaken in a special institute having its own autonomy. The primary objective of the institute is to perform a national service by preparing a limited number of well-qualified Americans to understand the Soviet Union and its people and as regional specialists to do work of authority and influence in business, in finance, in journalism, in various branches of government service, and in academic research and teaching in the social sciences and in literature.

The institute will attempt also to advance the general knowledge and understanding of that country, through research work and publications of its staff and of its students, and through the admission of students from other parts of the university to its general courses.

The two-year graduate program leading to a certificate of the institute is designed for students who wish to prepare themselves for scholarly or professional careers in the Russian field.

Within the institute, candidates will be expected to give special emphasis to one of five Russian fields: history, economy, government and law, international relations, or the social and ideological aspects of literature. Outside the institute, they will work simultaneously for an advanced degree in the graduate department or school of the university that is most closely allied with the specialty they elect within the institute. It is this double specialization which determines the requirements and procedure for admission of candidates and for granting the certificate of the institute.

Institution E

Regional concentrations are offered in this institution covering the following areas: Central Europe, France, Greece, Hispanic America, and the Pacific-Asiatic-Russian area.   In this regional concentration the student will study within the range of the language, literature, philosophy, arts, history, religion, social customs, governmental organization, and the cultural geography of one country or region.   The comprehensive plan of these regional studies will present attractive opportunities to students who wish to master, as far as time will permit, a comprehensive knowledge of some specific geographic and cultural area.   Typical of the regional concentration is the program for Pacific-Asiatic-Russian studies outlined below.

The specific objectives of the program are to give the student training in one of the languages, an over-all survey of the geography, peoples, history, politics, and cultures of the Pacific-Asiatic-Russian region, and a more intimate knowledge of a specific area.   Most of the subjects are to be taught by members of the School of Humanities, but there will be close collaboration with other schools and departments offering relevant subjects in order to provide a tightly knit program covering the essential topics.

At the present time the following languages are offered: Chinese (Mandarin), Japanese, Malay, and Russian; and the following areas will receive major attention: China, Japan, Russia, Southeast Asia, and the Pacific Islands.

Sixty quarter units will constitute a concentration in these studies.   Within this larger field each student may emphasize either language or area studies.

The various distributions of the total sixty units may be as follows:

a) A student wishing to emphasize area studies will take forty-five units of area studies and either (1) fifteen units of one of the languages related to the field of concentration, or (2) fifteen units in fields having a direct bearing upon the major program, such as anthropology, human geography, etc.

b) A student wishing to give more emphasis to language study may take thirty units of language and thirty units of area studies.

c) A student wishing to concentrate in Chinese, Japanese, or Russian language may take forty-five units of that language and select an additional fifteen units of area study related to his language field.

In his area studies, the student will choose, as he progresses, a field of concentration which may represent either a particular area (China, Japan, Russia, or Southeast Asia and Pacific Islands) or a comparative theme involving several related areas.

A planned program of twenty-five units of either language or area studies is offered as a possible minor for students majoring in other schools or departments. Students will be urged, where possible, to begin the study of one of the languages and to take both quarters of the introductory area course in the freshman or sophomore year.

This regional concentration aims to give a foundation in language, national culture and history, geography, economics, and social and political institutions to those who may want to continue, at a graduate level, training for specific positions in foreign countries during the postwar period.

Institution F

Institution F offers a program in Far Eastern studies, involving one general major and four specialized majors. All courses require a general survey course on problems relating to the Pacific, and in addition, the general major requires a further forty-five credits in Far Eastern studies, while the majors in Japanese, Chinese, and Slavic studies require thirty credits in the language and fifteen additional credits relative to the area. The major in Oriental languages requires, in addition, forty-five credits in languages and fifteen additional credits in the area. Though this institution has had for a number of years a Far Eastern program, the curriculum received a new impetus and a new sense of direction from the ASTP experience. All the languages will be taught by the intensive method and the area program will be arranged so as to provide a practical knowledge of present-day conditions in the countries under examination.

This civilian language and area training program will include such courses as Chinese or Japanese government, with strong emphasis on the practical details of local government; economic problems of Japan or China; courses dealing with the social institutions, customs, etiquette, population and hygiene problems of China, Japan, or Korea. These, together with instruction in the language and the historical and cultural background, should provide adequate training not only for students specializing in the field, but also for engineers, economists, and experts in other fields who may need to apply their professional knowledge in a specific Far Eastern country. It further believes that such a program offers in a general way a practical attempt to reorient the American attitude toward the countries of the Far East.

Institution G

At Institution G provision is made for a concentration in East Asia area and in Latin America on the undergraduate level, involving both an areal major and an areal minor. Requirements are at least twenty-four hours of upper-division work selected from a number of related courses. Certain introductory courses in government, history, economics, and sociology are also recommended, taken normally in the freshman and sophomore years. Students studying China will be required to take the Chinese language, two years of which are offered.

For the Latin-American concentration, basic courses in either Spanish or Portuguese, and in economics, American and European history, geography and government are considered as prerequisites. Required courses in upper division are prescribed in fulfillment of the concentration program.

Graduate study leading to the master of arts in Oriental affairs and in Latin-American affairs and leading to the doctor of philosophy in Oriental affairs is provided.

Institution H

At Institution H, provision is made for areal or regional majors in American civilization, Far East, China, Japan, France and the French colonies, Germany and Central Europe, Hispanic America, Russia and Eastern Europe. Graduate study and research are possible in the social sciences and languages in all of the above listed areas. Here, the major in Far Eastern studies is intended for students who seek a more thorough knowledge of the Far East than can be obtained by a major in any one department. The program is composed chiefly of courses in the social sciences dealing with Asia, the Far East, and the Pacific. Language study—Chinese, Japanese, or Russian—is included in the major. Concentration begins in the upper division, and twenty-four credits are required in geography, history, political science, economics, and anthropology, as basic courses; and twelve units are required in advanced anthropology, botany, economics, history, and courses in Oriental languages or Slavic languages.

The regional group majors were designed to combine studies in the geography, history, government, and ethnography of an important region or country with intensive study of the corresponding foreign language. The purpose of these regional majors is to afford a liberal education through an integrated group of courses, and at the same time to train persons for immediate tasks connected with military operations and occupations and for later relations between the United States and other nations. The total of upper-division credits in the regional major should normally be not less than thirty units.

A typical program for a regional group major on China would be:

Prerequisites

Elementary economics, geography, history, political science as basic courses and the study of Chinese begun in the lower division.

Requirements

One year of intensive training in Chinese leading to proficiency equal to reading a newspaper; geography, three units; history, six units; political science, nine units. Courses in anthropology, economics, and further courses in geography, history, and Oriental languages are recommended.

Institution I

At Institution I, provision is made for an areal major on Latin America, with plans under way for majors in Russian, African, and Oriental studies. Graduate study is provided in the following regions: Latin America, Africa, China, and India. Plans are being formulated toward a stronger integration of disciplines directed toward these areas.

Institution J

At Institution J, plans are being made to establish programs in Russian area, China, and eventually it is hoped that a program of Indic studies can be arranged. Language classes will be taught intensively, so that students may be able to study the corresponding area in the language itself. Considerable planning is under way for extension of area activities.

Institution K

At Institution K, an Interdepartmental Committee on Area Studies has been formed to advise on all matters pertaining to area programs. At present, provision is made for an areal major in Western Europe, Central Europe, Eastern Europe, the Far East, and Latin America. Programs for a minor concentration are also provided in all areas offered. It is hoped soon to establish Chinese language and literature courses at the university. Graduate work and research are possible in all areas, with the better qualified departments being history, political science, and European languages.

Institution L

Institution L has an already established committee on Latin-American studies in the College of Liberal Arts, but establishment of a general area committee in the graduate school is under consideration. At present, an areal major is provided for Latin America only. Considerable changes are under way for the creation of further area study programs. On the graduate level, research may be undertaken in political science with respect to the Far East, and in political science, history, and geography concerning Latin America.

FUTURE PLANS FOR AREA STUDY

The above listings and citations reveal that there is interest in a variety of programs dealing with area study both on the graduate and undergraduate level; and that provision has been made for the student to study "area" as an element in his general education, since he may enter these area courses even though he does not intend to major or minor in the area. It would seem, then, that area study is being conceived and planned to encompass a very wide group of divergent areas, in some cases within the individual institution, in others scattered among several, and that there is interest in these programs for general education as well as for specialized or vocational needs. It will also be seen that area study for the most part is limited, as must necessarily be the case, to the existing facilities required in any successful operation of the program.[3] Several institutions which are desirous of establishing an areal curriculum have this much in mind and realize that little, if anything, can be done until those facilities become available. It is possible that through timely grants from interested donors, and with perhaps some programs individually patronized by the foreign country concerned, a great deal may be done to acquire the requisite library materials needed to launch a really vital program of area studies on a broad and generally integrated basis. At least, the wartime areal programs showed the need for the establishment of areal programs and the existence of reference centers where all kinds of specialized information about a foreign country could be found. This fact alone should be a prime factor in the creation of sound area programs on a wide basis throughout the country.

[3] Cf. Maurice T. Price, "A Proposal for Foreign Area Courses," *Bulletin of the American Association of University Professors*, XXXI (1945), 648–67. A special treatment of minimum personnel, subject matter, and requirements.

Part Three

SIGNIFICANCE FOR THE FUTURE

XI. CONCLUSIONS AND IMPLICATIONS

THE LANGUAGE and area programs of the armed services developed certain aspects of educational theory long held by civilian educators and practised by them to some extent. But the huge resources of the armed services and the far-reaching demands of the war emergency enabled them to apply their educational theory with reference to language and area study on a vast and comprehensive scale.[1] In the course of this operation, methodologies were developed and results achieved that have considerable significance for the future of these studies in civilian education.

The language and area program did not continue long enough during the wartime period to show conclusively the soundness and the validity of the program for postwar education. This does not mean of course that such a program is entirely without implications for civilian education. The Army and Navy establishments were quickly planned, they were constantly in a state of flux and change, and the personnel assigned were often withdrawn before completion of the courses due to the exigencies of the war. Thus it is difficult to establish a sound basis on which a program of this kind might be judged. On the other hand, the programs are latent with a wealth of suggestive ideas. In general, the programs of the armed services went far to establish: (1) the validity of the oral approach to language study for practical purposes; (2) the fruitfulness of concentration on the study of an area; and (3) that certain educational gains are achieved by the intensive study of area and language in a combined program.

In any adaptation of these approaches and methodologies to the civilian study of area and language much can be learned from the experiences of the armed services. However, the objectives of universities and colleges are not the same as those of the wartime area programs. Because of their readily apparent utilitarian

---

[1] See Appendixes C and D for comparison of numbers of area and language trainees in relation to other phases of instruction, both with regard to demand and production.

emphasis, the wartime programs could not attempt to present a completely comprehensive and well-rounded education in the regions studied. It must be remembered that these programs were established with limited objectives in mind. From the point of view of the needs of the armed services the objectives were sound. The limitations that were necessarily imposed by the wartime emergency need not remain valid for area or language study for education on a peacetime basis.

The programs that were set up by the Army and Navy are full of suggestions for civilian institutions which serve other and additional ends. The integration of the separate academic disciplines into a common core of knowledge covering a cultural area or region, however difficult and beset with obstacles the process may be, is possible. The programs showed that at least for the practical needs they served, there is value in integration and in cooperation.

The development of the oral skills in language learning, with neglect of reading and grammar or embodying but a minimum of both, cannot be classified either as education or research in the general understanding of these terms, but it may be considered a means to these ends. To speak and understand a foreign language is a beneficial and useful art. Any intensive and thorough understanding of a foreign culture implies a reading knowledge of the language in which that culture finds expression, for chiefly there does one find the record of its realized ideals, its age-old traditions, and its cherished aspirations.

The practical ends of both language and area studies as demonstrated by the armed services in the several establishments described in this report would seem to place them on a vocational or "tool skill" level. Like all the training and educational programs of the Army and Navy, these studies were pursued in order that the trainee should perform a specific task. Proof of the value of these courses in this respect, then, would be best determined by showing how well the trainees were able to function in the tasks to which they were assigned as a result of the training which they received. There is at present no evidence on this subject, nor is it likely that reliable data will ever be available for general conclusions regarding the actual value of the programs in the subsequent war experience of the trainees.

In the study of languages, we must evaluate the gains and losses in the matter of intensification. Will the almost exclusive emphasis on the oral approach in language study prescribed by the armed services meet the traditional demands of language study in a liberal education, or ought a proportionate emphasis be placed on reading and writing? In area study, the experience of the armed services raises the question of whether or not the purely functional aspects of this type of concentration can be adapted to the purposes of a liberal education.

Finally, we must secure authoritative information on how financially feasible the intensive study of language is, with its emphasis on the use of numerous informants in very small classes and a high proportion of contact hours in civilian education. We must also raise the same question of expense respecting the adoption of an intensive and integrated study of area in civilian education.

In the following conclusions regarding implications of Army and Navy programs for postwar civilian education, it will be noted that many problems are still unsolved. Under the circumstances, more will be gained by pointing out those points on which experimentation is needed than by attempting to formulate conclusions which must be highly subjective. In educational matters it is easy to dogmatize, but the experienced administrator or teacher is not convinced by inferences based merely on the opinion of an investigator or investigators without experimental support. In the lack of such evidence, the only safe method is to point out the questions which still require an answer and indicate the fields where further experimentation is needed.

LANGUAGE STUDY

Interest

A great deal of interest has been stimulated in language and area study by the armed services programs. This applies to students and teachers and also to the general public. The subsequent organization of similar programs in the colleges and in the lower schools is an indication of their continuing appeal for civilian education. Nevertheless, there is need of further trial and experimentation before any final decision can be reached that the oral approach should supplement, or supplant, the traditional grammar-reading approach.

Objectives

Just as the objectives were clearly defined for the wartime programs, so they must be for peacetime. Again, the methods employed should be directly aimed at the attainment of the objectives. Should peacetime objectives be limited to almost sole emphasis on speaking and understanding, or should they include the skills of reading and writing? Should we include a larger measure of oral emphasis than heretofore, while maintaining grammatical thoroughness? Or, should we use the oral approach, as a matter of interest, as the best method of introducing the student to language study? Should language study emphasize the "tool skill" value, or should it be related to a broader cultural perspective? Whatever objectives are desired or prescribed, we must understand that we will achieve what we emphasize.

Intensive courses

Intensive courses for the armed services programs meant fifteen or eighteen, sometimes more, hours of study per week. What should be the time normally prescribed for intensive or semi-intensive courses in the postwar curriculum? The intensive course needs further definition in its relation to home study, supervised study, scheduling of classes, and the like. It is to be expected, of course, that more time spent in study of any subject will bring more and better results. If any study becomes increasingly intensive, however, is there not a saturation point beyond which the returns diminish in relation to the time devoted to it? What is this time limit? In the study of language, how can we evaluate the gain or loss by intensification over a shorter period of time? Will the intensive courses have the same value for later recall of knowledge once learned as the nonintensive courses? May not the whole attempt of the armed services to intensify a course of study and thus shorten its normal span prove to be a fallacy when applied generally to civilian conditions?

Oral inductive method

The wartime intensive course in the Navy was designed for complete basic training in all aspects of the language, and thus served to provide a basis for further cultural development. The purpose was to equip the student with the whole language and was not limited to the tool-skill level or to oral-aural drill and practice. The language programs of the Army placed almost exclusive emphasis on the oral inductive approach, so that the trainee would acquire a rather fluent speaking knowledge of the language and a nearly perfect aural comprehension of it as well. This was done by "mim-mem" drills, using informants, or native speakers of the language, and approximates more or less the "natural approach." Can these features be adapted to, and are they desirable for, civilian education? If it can be determined that the development of the oral skills has the same value for general education as it has for the acquisition of a tool serving a specific and immediate need, these features may eventually be adopted.

Results

For the armed services, the real test of whether or not an individual trainee had received the proper and requisite training rested upon his ability to perform the task for which he was trained. For the liberal arts program any such pragmatic test is out of the question. We can rely only on objective testing data which can show beyond doubt the superiority of one set of methodologies over another. Is there any carry-over value from the oral-aural intensive method to acquisition of ability in reading or grammar? This raises many questions, and much testing will be required. Can reading, writing and grammar be more readily or more effectively learned after an introductory oral approach? What is the rate of subsequent deterioration through disuse when the oral approach is emphasized solely? Constant control of results will be necessary in order to place students in classes best suited to their ability. This is particularly difficult when the oral skills are concerned, and at present, the techniques for objective testing of oral skills are in the experimental stage.

Does intensive training get the student to use the language naturally and spontaneously, as no other method can? The study of a language should be related to a broad cultural perspective. But can this be opened up until the student has acquired a practical working knowledge of the language? Peripheral and tangential association with a language by means of discussion in English is a surface-scratching illusion which can be corrected only by giving the student a prior mastery of the language sufficient to enable him to work directly in it and not indirectly around the edges of it. The student of a language should learn to think in it as soon as possible.

Selection and motivation of students

The basis of selection for trainees in the wartime programs cannot be used in civilian education. It is possible that the results claimed in the wartime intensive language programs were achieved because the personnel were specially selected and highly motivated. Attempts were made to place trainees in small classes gauged to their ability. How should students be selected for language study in the intensive courses? Should there be no special screening and the student be allowed to choose for himself? Should the language requirement for graduation in school and college be abolished? If the language requirement is abolished, will there not be, perhaps, more good students desiring to study foreign languages?

Training of teachers and in-service training

The wartime programs revealed the lack of properly trained teachers even for the more commonly taught languages. Linguists and informants, usually native speakers of the language, were used for the languages (rarely studied) because other teachers were not available. Many of these, some of whom were refugees, had to be trained while in service. There is need to study the present program of teacher-training in languages if the oral approach is to receive any degree of recognition, especially in the lower schools. In-service training, as well as pre-service training, will be needed for the satisfaction of the needs of the oral technique.

Teaching materials and aids

The language and area programs were supplemented by the use of numerous training aids on a much wider scale than is true for civilian education. These were geared to wartime needs. New texts, basic vocabularies, audio-visual aids, mechanical devices, and all sorts of technical equipment will need to be developed for peacetime objectives. A careful study needs to be made of their most beneficial and practical use. Classroom materials of the above types geared to peacetime needs will have to be prepared. Texts and vocabularies should be prepared containing an abundance of cultural material relating to the region where the language is spoken. These new texts will not be intended to teach the grammar of the language solely, but will be of a type for simultaneous study of the language and the common, everyday experiences of the foreign people whose civilization and customs are as much worth knowing as their language.

Planned environment—language houses

For a generally intensive program, language houses approximating or simulating the foreign atmosphere should be planned and established. In institutions where this feature is not possible, language tables, dramatics clubs, song fests, or any other outside activity can be created to provide incentives for the study of the language. This is one way to provide motivation, since the student will find through this medium an opportunity to use the language as he continues to learn it.

Russian and Far Eastern languages

The wartime program showed the need for and created an interest in the study of the lesser known languages, such as Russian, Chinese, Japanese, Arabic, Malay, etc. The gains that were made in this direction should not be lost in the postwar period. Because of the peculiar complexity of Oriental writing systems, it seems logical that extreme emphasis be placed on the spoken idiom, in the early stages. How long should the oral emphasis continue and should writing and reading be delayed in these languages even longer than may be advisable for the Western European languages?

Supervision and coordination of classes

Close supervision over the progress of the program was necessary for the wartime language programs in order to attain the objectives. This supervision also aided in improving the instruction and in assuring proper coordination between analysis classes and the drill sessions. Supervision over large numbers of beginning classes is needed to evaluate the relative rate of progress, the level of attainment, and to assure the achievement of the same subject-matter content by the several sections of an entire class program, such as first year, first term, and so on.

Traditional and intensive courses

Should traditional and intensive courses be offered in an institution, possibly paralleling each other? If so, on what basis will students be chosen for either course? Will the students be allowed their own choice? How can the problem of granting credit for the intensive courses be solved? Is there not a basis such as exists for chemistry or zoology laboratory classes by which the proper credit, neither too much nor too little, is granted? Will the students electing the intensive courses be able to fulfill the language requirements, or will the language requirements have to be changed to suit the intensive courses? Can the intensive classes properly equip the student to enter the later literature classes? On this point it is noted that all students in the later phases of the intensive language courses in the Navy read and studied standard literary works of the countries concerned. Until the foregoing questions have been answered by concrete objective data, no final conclusions can be reached.

AREA STUDY

Integrated area study

The idea of area study, though a feature of prewar education, gained widespread recognition during the war. The language guides, pocket guides, war-background studies, and the civil-affairs handbooks which were distributed in great numbers, as well as the intensive study in language and area by a selected few, did much to change the outlook of the soldier-citizen toward the rest of the world. Area study was greatly developed during the war, since little known regions were stressed for the first time. Emphasis in these wartime programs was contemporaneous rather than historical; the approach was functional rather than developmental. Can the purely functional aspects of the type of concentration on an area which existed in the wartime programs have value for, or be adapted to, the purposes of a liberal education? Is a knowledge of the area to be regarded as an end in itself as in Army or Navy practice? Should it be regarded as background material for a concentration on some particular discipline connected with the area such as history, economics, or social institutions? Will there be sufficient scholarly materials to carry on an area-study program if area study is undertaken from the cultural rather than the practical viewpoint? What is to be the unit or size of the area under examination? Is it to be limited to the area where one major language is spoken? What are to be the regions designated for treatment in the so-called area-study programs?

Interdepartmental cooperation and centralized organization

During the war the area program was administered effectively by an informal interdepartmental committee with one of the members acting as director. Associate directors were appointed in charge of single areas. To achieve the objective and to present adequately the desired subject-matter content, faculty members representing a wide range of academic disciplines were urged to cooperate in a measure beyond the limits of accepted academic practice. Should area study, comprising all areas, be under one director or coordinator? Should each area have its own director? Should the directors chosen have complete authority over the area program as in wartime practice? What is the best type of organization for area study in civilian institutions? Should control be centralized or departmentalized? In area study during the war, the participating disciplines were forged into an integrated program with the courses presented concurrently or sometimes in sequence. How will integration best be achieved for civilian needs once it is realized that the time element is no longer a critical factor? Will the idea of concurrent courses, such as the wartime programs sometimes exemplified for the sake of expediency, have practical value for peacetime education? For a four-year college program or for the long period required for graduate study, the practices obtaining during the war may be inadvisable.

Graduate or undergraduate levels, degrees, and credits

If area study is to be introduced on a wider scale in the college curriculum, is it possible to establish an adequate areal program, accompanied by language study, on the undergraduate level? Could an undergraduate major in the area and language be regarded as a preparation for future specialized graduate work in the area? Should a vocational minor in area be introduced into the college program? To what degree should the area study program lead? How will the matter of credits be determined? Will there be a specified over-all number for the specific area or a minimum number for each participating discipline? Can an adequate area program be established on the graduate level leading to both the M.A. and the Ph.D.? Or should the prewar practice of regarding area study as background material continue, with the advanced degree to be given in the discipline of concentration connected with the area?

Teaching materials

The wartime area programs revealed lacunae with respect to materials not only in the less familiar region, but also in lands whose cultural patterns more or less parallel our own. Materials should be prepared which are properly organized, adequate, and scholarly. With special reference to the undergraduate level, should these materials be prepared on the basis of departmentalized units, or should they be prepared with the intent of encompassing the entire area?

Integration of language and area

The wartime programs called for concurrent courses in language and area. Should this feature be continued in postwar civilian education? Should we insist that the student first obtain a knowledge of the language through intensive methods and then apply it to the area? Materials prepared in the foreign language could then be used and would present an interpretation of history and the general culture as commonly taught and accepted in the area itself.

Possibilities for general education—substitution of broad survey courses for the piecemeal curriculum [2]

In an effort to make the first two years of college more comprehensive in scope and more stimulating in appeal, some colleges have substituted for the old-time piecemeal curriculum broad survey courses in the fields of science, the social studies, and the humanities. Here the whole field has supplanted the separate subject. The Army area-study classes were trained in comprehensive understanding of the area to which students were to be assigned, with the realization that they would not be able to solve the many problems to be encountered unless they were equipped with this broad, basic, and integrated knowledge. In imitation of these programs, some colleges may make similar plans for the liberal education of their students. The idea of intensive single courses like the language program of the ASTP may have merit for other academic subjects. The area-study program may pave the way for further types of integrated courses, possibly dealing with one's own civilization and culture, to which that of foreign and past cultures can be related in terms of mutual or general enlightenment. Both would include physical factors, the framework of important historical events, the chief political, economic, and social problems, great literary and artistic expression, and the scientific, philosophical, and religious interpretations of life. An integrated areal program, based on a modern cultural region, might go far to provide the advantages of the old liberal arts courses centered about classical civilization.

Utilitarian aspects of area study

An exploration of the various needs in the fields of government, business, and missionary endeavors, especially in the lesser known areas, needs to be made as a basis for the determination of establishing suitable vocational programs. Should vocational

[2] Cf. Walter L. Agard, "Liberal Education after the War," *Journal of Higher Education*, XVI (February 1945), 57–62.

programs in area be established once a market is found in which the trained areal specialist can apply his knowledge?

Cooperation among institutions and experts

Colleges and universities now engaged in offering area-study programs, or planning to do so, should cooperate to prevent waste through duplication in staffing and library purchases beyond the basic needs of introductory courses. Such cooperation will influence the flow of students to the best sources for specific ends of training and the application of their knowledge.[3] Interchange of areal experts among the colleges and universities may also become a desirable feature. A clearing house of materials and sources should also be established to assure proper distribution and exchange of the limited materials now available. Universities which have the facilities should establish special divisions for the preparation of teaching materials and personnel for area study in the little known or little explored regions.

In conclusion, reference should be made again to the introductory statement respecting the necessity for experimentation in adapting to civilian ends in education the massive effort of the Army and Navy in the fields of language and area study. Without such undertakings on the part of universities, colleges, and secondary schools the program patterns of the armed services cannot be made effective for the shaping of peacetime courses, and the important initiative will fail of implementation and gradually deteriorate both in psychological effect and methodological usefulness. In the field of language, as has been shown, certain projects are already in progress in the colleges and the secondary schools. In the field of area study some experimental integrated area programs also exist. It is the plain duty of teachers and administrators to face boldly and energetically the task of finding answers to the questions that remain unsolved and seeking ways to overcome the difficulties that stand in the path of further efforts in this direction.

[3] Cf. "A Review of Far Eastern and Slavic Studies in Five Institutions of the Western States, 1944" (Rockefeller Foundation, Humanities Division, New York, N. Y.), p. 2.

APPENDIX A

INSTITUTIONS OFFERING ASTP AREA AND LANGUAGE INSTRUCTION

Amherst College	French, German, Italian, Spanish
Bard College	French, German
Boston College	French, German, Spanish
Boston University	French, German, Italian
California, University of (Berkeley)	German, Italian, Russian, Serbo-Croat, Chinese, Japanese, Thai
California, University of (Los Angeles)	German, Italian, Chinese
Carleton College	French, German
Carnegie Institute of Technology	French, German, Spanish
Chicago, University of	French, German, Italian, Russian, Chinese, Japanese
Cincinnati, University of	French, German, Spanish
Clark University	German, Greek, Italian
College of the City of New York	French, German, Italian, Russian, Spanish
Cornell University	Czech, German, Italian, Russian, Chinese
Denver, University of	Bulgarian, French, German, Hungarian, Japanese
Fordham University	French, German, Italian, Spanish
Georgetown University	French, German, Italian, Russian, Spanish, Chinese, Japanese
Grinnell College	German, Italian, Spanish
Hamilton College	French, German
Harvard University	German, Russian, Chinese, Japanese
Haverford College	German, Italian
Idaho, University of	French, German, Russian
Illinois, University of	French, German, Italian, Spanish
Indiana University	Bulgarian, German, Greek, Hungarian, Polish, Russian, Serbo-Croat, Turkish
Iowa, State University of	Czech, German, Italian
Johns Hopkins University	French, German, Italian
Kenyon College	French, German
Lafayette College	French, German, Italian, Spanish
Lehigh University	French, German
Maryland, University of	French, German, Spanish
Michigan State College of Agriculture and Applied Science	French, German, Italian, Spanish

Michigan, University of	French, German, Italian, Persian, Spanish, Japanese
Minnesota, University of	Finnish, German, Norwegian, Swedish, Japanese
Missouri, University of	German, Italian, Russian
Nebraska, University of	German
New York University	French, German, Russian
North Carolina, University of	French, German, Italian, Spanish
Ohio State University	German, Italian, Spanish
Oregon State College	French, German, Russian, Spanish, Chinese
Oregon, University of	Italian, Norwegian, Portuguese, Russian, Spanish
Pennsylvania, University of	Arabic, German, Russian, Bengali, Chinese, Hindustani
Pittsburgh, University of	German, Greek, Russian, Serbo-Croat
Pomona College	French, Spanish, Chinese, Japanese
Princeton University	Arabic, French, German, Italian, Spanish, Turkish
Queens College	French, German, Spanish
Rutgers University	French, German, Italian, Spanish
St. Louis University	German, Italian
Stanford University	Dutch, French, German, Italian, Russian, Spanish, Chinese, Japanese, Malayan
Syracuse University	French, German, Russian, Spanish
Utah, University of	German, Italian, Spanish, Japanese
Vanderbilt University	French, German
Washington, University of	Chinese, Japanese, Korean
Washington University (St. Louis)	German, Italian
Wisconsin, University of	German, Italian, Norwegian, Polish, Portuguese, Russian, Spanish
Wyoming, University of	French, German, Spanish
Yale University	Italian, Russian, Burmese, Chinese, Japanese, Malayan

APPENDIX B

FOREIGN AREA AND LANGUAGE CURRICULA

CURRICULUM 0-2
LINGUISTIC FIELDS

Effective: 12 June 1943

Superseded by Curriculum 96 Linguistic Fields (Effective: 8 November 1943)

Term 9L

Refresher and orientation training for trainees overqualified for the most advanced regular ASTP curricula in Foreign Area and Languages. The curriculum prescribes a minimum of 24 contact hours a week in a foreign language and in the geography and the social, political, and economic institutions of the corresponding foreign area. The time devoted to each subject is prescribed by the institution to complement the varying backgrounds of the trainees. Language instruction is refresher training for men already competent in the foreign language. Area instruction is at an advanced level for trainees overqualified for regular area courses. Approximately 24 hours a week of independent study are required. Course descriptions are not provided for this curriculum.

CURRICULUM 71
FOREIGN AREA AND LANGUAGE STUDIES
Term 7L

Effective: 8 May 1944

	TOTAL CONTACT HOURS A WEEK	RECOMMENDED DISTRIBUTION	
Term 7L			
Language Study: AST–218......................	18	3	15
Area Study: AST–268........................	6	6	0
Total.................................	24	9	15

NOTE.—It is expected that a number of hours equal to the number of contact hours will be devoted to outside study.

179

CURRICULUM 72
LINGUISTIC FIELDS

Effective: 13 December 1943

Special Term 4

A curriculum for trainees competent in a foreign language but without special knowledge of the corresponding foreign area. The curriculum prescribes the equivalent of 24 contact hours of instruction in a foreign language and in the geography and the social, political, and economic institutions of the corresponding foreign area. The time devoted to each subject is prescribed by the institution to complement the varying backgrounds of trainees. Language instruction is refresher training for men already competent in the foreign language. Area instruction is at the level of Curriculum 71. Instruction is by means of conference, class, laboratory, seminary, and specific projects at the discretion of the institution. Approximately 24 hours a week of independent study are required.

CURRICULUM 71
FOREIGN AREA AND LANGUAGE STUDIES

Effective: 11 October 1943

COURSE	TOTAL CONTACT HOURS A WEEK	RECOMMENDED DISTRIBUTION	
		Class	Lab.
Term 4			
Language Study: AST–215............................	15	3	12
Area Study: AST–265................................	8	8	0
Contemporary History, 1914 to the Present: AST–201...	2	2	0
Total..	25	13	12
Term 5			
Language Study: AST–216............................	15	3	12
Area Study: AST–266................................	8	8	0
Contemporary History, 1914 to the Present: AST–202...	2	2	0
Total..	25	13	12
Term 6			
Language Study: AST–217............................	15	3	12
Area Study: AST–267................................	8	8	0
Contemporary History, 1914 to the Present: AST–203...	2	2	0
Total..	25	13	12

NOTE 1.—Institutions are authorized to make such minor changes in the allocation of hours as local conditions seem to warrant.

NOTE 2.—It is expected that a number of hours equal to the number of contact hours will be devoted to outside study.

CURRICULUM 73
FOREIGN AREA AND LANGUAGE STUDIES

Prerequisite: Successful completion of ASTRP Curriculum B-80
Effective: 11 September 1944

COURSE	TOTAL CONTACT HOURS A WEEK	RECOMMENDED DISTRIBUTION		STUDY HOURS A WEEK
		Class	Lab.	
Term 4L				
Area Study 81 (Customs and Social Institutions)..	8	8	0	8
Language Study 83..........................	15	3	12	12
Total...................................	23	11	12	20

CURRICULUM 96
LINGUISTIC FIELDS

Effective: 8 November 1943

Term 9L

A restatement of Curriculum 0-2 with minor revisions.

Refresher and orientation training for trainees overqualified for the most advanced regular ASTP curricula in Foreign Area and Languages. The curriculum prescribes a minimum of 24 contact hours a week in a foreign language and in the geography and the social, political, and economic institutions of the corresponding foreign area. The time devoted to each subject is prescribed by the institution to complement the varying backgrounds of the trainees. Language instruction is refresher training for men already competent in the foreign language. Area instruction is at an advanced level for trainees overqualified for regular area courses. Approximately 24 hours a week of independent study are required.

CURRICULUM 704
FOREIGN AREA AND LANGUAGE STUDIES
"B" Plan

Effective: 12 June 1943   Superseded by Curriculum 71
                                             (Effective: 8 May 1944)

COURSE	TOTAL CONTACT HOURS A WEEK	RECOMMENDED DISTRIBUTION	
		Class	Lab.
Term 4			
Language Study: AST–756.........................	17	5	12
Area Study, Geographical Aspects: AST–710..........	10	10	0
Total...	27	15	12

CURRICULUM 704—*Continued*

COURSE	TOTAL CONTACT HOURS A WEEK	RECOMMENDED DISTRIBUTION	
		Class	Lab.
Term 5			
Language Study: AST–757............................	17	5	12
Area Study, Historical Aspects: AST–711..............	10	10	0
Total...	27	15	12
Term 6			
Language Study: AST–758...........................	17	5	12
Area Study, Institutional and Cultural Aspects: AST–712.	10	10	0
Total...	27	15	12

NOTE.—It is expected that a number of hours equal to the number of contact hours will be devoted to outside study.

CURRICULUM 705

FOREIGN AREA AND LANGUAGE STUDIES

Effective: 13 April 1943   Superseded by Curriculum 71 (Effective: 8 May 1944)

COURSE	TOTAL CONTACT HOURS A WEEK	PRESCRIBED DISTRIBUTION	
		Class	Lab.
Term 4			
Area Study: AST–706.............................	12	12	0
Modern History and Contemporary World Affairs: AST–134...................................	4	4	0
Language Study: AST–755..........................	13	6	7
Police Science and Law Enforcement: AST–912.........	1	1	0
Total...	30	23	7

Term 5

The work of Term 5 in Foreign Area and Language Studies is a continuation of the work of Term 4.

Term 6

The work of Term 6 in Foreign Area and Language Studies is a continuation of the work of Term 5.

NOTE.—It is expected that a number of hours equal to the number of contact hours will be devoted to outside study.

CURRICULUM

JAPANESE TRANSLATOR

Special Term 4

Effective: 13 September 1943

A curriculum to prepare specially selected trainees for further training in a service-school program of instruction which presupposes some competence in reading Japanese. The curriculum prescribes approximately 18 hours of instruction a week in Japanese and approximately 24 hours of study a week. The time is devoted to intensive instruction and practice in reading and writing Japanese. Course descriptions are not provided for this curriculum.

Language Study 81

First of sequence of three intensive courses in Japanese with special emphasis upon development of conversational skill; same objectives as Language Study: AST-215. 3 class, 12 laboratory hours (devoted to drill in the spoken language), 12 study hours; Term 2, Curriculum B-80.

Language Study 82

Sequent to Language Study 81. 3 class, 12 laboratory hours (devoted to drill in the spoken language), 10 study hours; Term 3, Curriculum B-80.

Language Study 83

Sequent to Language Study 82. 3 class, 12 laboratory hours (devoted to drill in the spoken language) ; Term 4, Curriculum 73.

Language Study: AST-215

First of sequence of three courses in modern foreign language; special emphasis on colloquial spoken form of the language: to develop ability to speak fluently, accurately, and with acceptable approximation of native pronunciation, and to develop complete auditory comprehension of the language as spoken by natives; intensive instruction and practice in one of the following languages: Annamese, Arabic (Moroccan, Syrian), Bengali, Bulgarian, Burmese, Chinese (Cantonese, Foochow, Fukien, Mandarin), Czech, Dutch, Finnish, French, German, Greek, Hindustani, Hungarian, Italian, Japanese, Korean, Malayan, Norwegian, Polish, Portuguese, Persian, Russian, Serbo-Croatian, Spanish, Swedish, Thai, Turkish. 3 class, 12 laboratory hours (devoted to drill in the spoken language) ; Term 4, Curriculum 71.

Language Study: AST-216

Sequent to Language Study: AST-215. 3 class, 12 laboratory hours (devoted to drill in the spoken language) ; Term 5, Curriculum 71.

Language Study: AST-217

Sequent to Language Study: AST-216. 3 class, 12 laboratory hours (devoted to drill in the spoken language) ; Term 6, Curriculum 71.

Language Study: AST-218

Sequent to Language Study: AST-217. 3 class, 15 laboratory hours (devoted to drill in the spoken language) ; Term 7L, Curriculum 71.

Language Study: AST-755

Three-term course; same content as Language Study: AST-215-6-7. 6 class, 7 laboratory hours (devoted to drill in the spoken language) ; continuous through Terms 4, 5, 6, Curriculum 705.

Language Study: AST-756

First of sequence of courses in a modern foreign language; same content as Language Study: AST-215. 5 class, 12 laboratory hours (devoted to drill in the spoken language), Term 4, Curriculum 704.

Language Study: AST-757

Sequent to Language Study: AST-756. 5 class, 12 laboratory hours (devoted to drill in the spoken language) ; Term 5, Curriculum 704.

Language Study: AST-758

Sequent to Language Study: AST-757. 5 class, 12 laboratory hours (devoted to drill in the spoken language) ; Term 6, Curriculum 704.

Area Study 81

Course for foreign language students; customs and social institutions of area in which language is spoken; vital statistics; public health and sanitation; domestic economy; folkways; religious institutions; class and caste division; education; popular and classical literature; popular amusements and sports; facilities and character of public information; current economic and political situation; relation of civilian to military. 8 class, 8 study hours; Term 4L, Curriculum 73.

Area Study: AST-265

First of sequence of three courses for students of a foreign language; geography, history, and the contemporary social, political, and economic institutions of the area in which the language is spoken; the three elements, geography, history, and contemporary institutions, may be presented sequentially or concurrently in the three terms; geography: climate, land forms, water supply, vegetation, types of animal life, natural resources, accessibility of the area, facilities for travel and communication, ethnic and linguistic origins and survivals, migrations; history: chronology of important events, growth of national sentiment and political organization, boundary questions and rivalries, religious institutions, technological, commercial, industrial, and agrarian development, legal and governmental institutions, international relationships, military history, important historical figures, cultural influence; contemporary institutions: vital statistics, public health and sanitation, domestic economy, folkways, religious institutions, class and caste divisions, education, popular and classical literature, popular amusements and sports, facilities and character of public information, current economic and political situation, relation of civilian to military. 8 class hours; Term 4, Curriculum 71.

Area Study: AST-266

Sequent to Area Study: AST-265. 8 class hours; Term 5, Curriculum 71.

Area Study: AST-267

Sequent to Area Study: AST-266. 8 class hours; Term 6, Curriculum 71.

Area Study: AST-268

Sequent to Area Study: AST-267; conducted in the language of the area. 6 class hours; Term 7L, Curriculum 71.

Area Study: AST-706

Three-term course in geography, history, and the social, political, and economic institutions of a foreign area; same content as Area Study: AST-265-6-7. 12 class hours; Term 4, 5, 6, Curriculum 705.

Area Study, Geographical Aspects: AST-710

First of sequence of three courses in geography, history, and the social, political, and economic institutions of a foreign area; same content as Area Study: AST-265-6-7; in AST-710 emphasis is on geography of the area. 10 class hours; Term 4, Curriculum 704.

Area Study, Historical Aspects: AST-711

Sequent to Area Study: AST-710; emphasis on history. 10 class hours; Term 5, Curriculum 704.

Area Study, Institutional and Cultural Aspects : AST-712

Sequent to Area Study: AST-711; emphasis on contemporary social, political, and economic institutions. 10 class hours; Term 6, Curriculum 704.

APPENDIX C

SUMMARY OF ASTP DEMANDS*

January 1943—July 1944

BY CURRICULA

	1943				1944		
	1 Jan.	April	July	Oct.	Jan.	April	July
Basic Phase							
General Basic........	....	10,231	45,770	15,450	32,541	....	....
Surveying..........	....	3,629	4,329	2,806	3,146	....	....
Int. Comb. Eng.....	....	6,476	8,185	5,518	7,218	....	....
Communications....	....	9,267	22,153	18,252	8,974	....	....
Acoustics & Optics..	....	1,289	1,589	997	997	....	....
Advanced Phase							
Area & Language....	1,745	4,056	9,695	11,262	11,481	2,725	2,725
Chemical..........	1,688	1,688	265	265	260	235	235
Civil.............	3,114	5,374	6,075	3,162	2,452	1,683	1,683
Electrical.........	5,638	9,811	8,615	6,368	5,413	3,043	3,043
Mechanical........	3,897	6,727	9,760	4,218	3,028	1,045	1,045
Personnel Psych......	1,170	1,170	1,100	1,100	....	....	....
Petroleum..........	....	....	....	....	....	70	70
Sanitary...........	584	584	360	360	270	215	215
Transportation......	....	....	50	50	....	....	....
Field Immaterial.....	....	4,529	5,329	3,502	....	....	....
Medicine..........	4,200	4,200	4,200	4,200	4,200	4,200	4,200
Dentistry..........	1,100	1,100	1,100	1,100	1,100	1,100	1,100
Veterinary.........	150	150	150	150	150	150	150
Total..........	23,286	70,281	128,725	78,760	81,230	14,466	14,466

* Signed by Francis M. Fitts, Colonel, M. C., Chief, Curricula and Standards Branch, ASF, Military Training Office, 30 September 1944.

APPENDIX D

SUMMARY OF ASTP PRODUCTION REPORTS*

NUMBERS SEPARATED FROM TERMS ENDING JUNE 1943 THROUGH DECEMBER 1945

CURRICULUM	TOTAL SEPARATED	SEPARATED PRIOR TO END OF TERM		SEPARATED AT END OF TERM								
				Total		Graduates		Failures		Others	
		No.	%	No.	%	No.	%	No.	%	No.	%
Basic											
General Basic................BE-1	93,732	19,817	21.1	73,915	78.9	20,282	21.6	21,511	22.9	32,122	34.3
Surveying...................BE-2	1,244	188	15.1	1,056	84.9	273	21.9	261	21.0	522	42.0
Internal Comb. Engine.......BE-3	1,076	177	16.4	899	83.6	220	20.4	316	29.4	363	33.7
Communications.............BE-4	1,088	223	20.5	865	79.5	146	13.4	269	24.7	450	41.4
Acoustics & Optics..........BE-5	243	54	22.2	189	77.8	42	17.3	29	11.9	118	48.6
Refresher......................R	429	125	29.1	304	70.9	0	0.0	228	53.1	76	17.7
Total Basic.............	97,812	20,584	21.0	77,228	79.0	20,963	21.4	22,614	23.1	33,651	34.4
Engineering											
Marine Transportation........	48	1	2.1	47	97.9	47	97.9	0	0.0	0	0.0
Engineering, E-1..............	293	37	12.6	256	87.4	0	0.0	200	68.3	56	19.1
Engineering (Inc. Uncl. 9A's)..	5,045	871	17.3	4,174	82.7	2,349	46.6	711	14.1	1,114	22.1
Chemical Engineering..........	1,106	172	15.6	934	84.4	468	42.3	138	12.5	328	29.7
Civil Engineering.............	5,229	492	9.4	4,737	90.6	1,805	34.5	860	16.4	2,072	39.6
Electrical Engineering.........	8,068	810	10.0	7,258	90.0	3,170	39.3	1,166	14.5	2,922	36.2
Mechanical Engineering........	7,046	591	8.4	6,455	91.6	2,334	33.1	689	9.8	3,432	48.7
Petroleum Engineering.........	9	0	0.0	9	100.0	9	100.0	0	0.0	0	0.0
Sanitary Engineering..........	397	22	5.5	375	94.5	363	91.4	12	3.0	0	0.0
Total Engineering........	27,241	2,996	11.0	24,245	89.0	10,545	38.7	3,776	13.9	9,924	36.4
Area & Language (Inc. 9L's)..	16,307	2,457	15.1	13,850	84.9	9,392	57.6	952	5.8	3,506	21.5
Preprofessional.............	2,354	361	15.3	1,993	84.7	0	0.0	541	23.0	1,452	61.7
Personnel Psychology........	1,354	72	5.3	1,282	94.7	1,181	87.2	43	3.2	58	4.3
Total..................	145,068	26,470	18.2	118,598	81.8	42,081	29.0	27,926	19.2	48,591	33.5

* Same source as preceding table.

187

BIBLIOGRAPHY

GENERAL REFERENCES

AGARD, FREDERICK B. "Aspects of Oral Testing," *French Review*, XIX (May 1946), 423–27.

Explanation of tests for aural comprehension with reference to French as prepared by the University of Chicago Language Investigation.

——. "Language Lessons War Has Taught," *Virginia Journal of Education*, XXXVIII (February 1945), 230–42.

Discusses the ASTP and how it can be incorporated into high school and college programs. This will require better trained teachers who can speak the foreign tongue, smaller classes, more time, etc.

——. "Reply to Professor Herman's Article on the ASTP," *Modern Language Journal*, XXIX (October 1945), 495–97.

Defends the ASTP language survey and claims the real purpose of the investigation was to describe and appraise what had been accomplished and to stimulate interest in adapting certain ASTP features to civilian classes.

AGARD, WALTER R. "Liberal Education after the War," *Journal of Higher Education*, XVI (February 1945), 57–62.

The author recalls the curriculum of the Experimental College, University of Wisconsin, and draws upon experience in the Army Area Studies to suggest in broad outlines a course of study for the American liberal arts college.

ANDERSON, HAROLD A. "A Report on Language Teaching in the Army," *School Review*, LII (October 1944), 458–60.

Discussion of the ASTP language survey published by the Commission on Trends in Education.

ANGIOLILLO, A. *Armed Forces Foreign Language Teaching.* New York, N. Y.: F. F. Vanni Publications, 30 W. Twelfth St., New York, N. Y. In press.

"The Army Has no Magic Formula for Learning Languages," *American Teacher*, XXVIII (March 1944), 22.

Discusses features of the ASTP language program. Points out that some of these may be retained in colleges after the war.

"Army Language Program for Enlisted Personnel," *French Review*, XVII (February 1944), 243–46.

A factual report of the language interest of the general public and particularly a description of the Foreign Area and Language courses of the ASTP and uses of men trained in these courses.

"Army Methods in Foreign Languages Adapted for Civilian Students," *School and Society*, LIX (May 6, 1944), 324–25.

Discussion of new programs in colleges influenced by the ASTP challenge.

ARNDT, C. O. "Far Eastern Studies in American Schools and Teachers' Colleges," *Bulletin of the National Association of Secondary School Principals of the NEA*, XXIX (May 1945), 11.

Discusses several surveys made on the place of Far Eastern studies in American schools and colleges, with conclusions and proposals for curriculum building.

AXELROD, JOSEPH. "The Navy Language School Program and Foreign Languages in Schools and Colleges: Aims and Techniques," *Modern Language Journal*, XXIX (January 1945), 40–47.

————. "The Navy Language School and College Foreign Language Departments: Personnel and Organization," *Modern Language Journal*, XXIX (February 1945), 127–32.

Description of Navy Oriental Language School curriculum, methods, and procedure, with reference to adoption by civilian educators. See section on this school in the report.

BABER, RAY E. "Sociologists and the Army Language and Area Studies," *Research Studies, State College of Washington*, XIII (1945), 25–32.

Discusses the Army language and area studies from the viewpoint of adoption, with suggested topics as possible area-study projects.

BERGEL, KURT. "German Conversation in the Army Specialized Training Program," *German Quarterly*, XVII (November 1944), 205–8.

Reports personal experiences, procedures, and the reaction of an informant at Stanford University.

BERRETT, D. S., ELLIS, FRANCIS H., ITTNER, R. T., and WOOLEY, E. O. "Report on Special Sections in Elementary German at Indiana University," *German Quarterly*, XIX (January 1946), 18–28.

Report on three elementary sections in German, involving (1) Army methods, (2) conversational and direct methods, and (3) grammar-reading method; descriptions of methods used; contains test scores and explanations, and conclusions.

BEYER, L. R. "University of Illinois Reports on Its Language Teaching Program," *School and Society*, LX (November 18, 1944), 325–26.

Lays stress on oral mastery. Points out that oral language must not be carried to the extreme of producing "foreign-language illiterates."

BLOCH, BERNARD, and TRAEGER, GEORGE L. *Outline of Linguistic Analysis*. Washington: Linguistic Society of America, 1942. Pp. 82.

Booklet was prepared to present in brief summary the techniques of analysis which are necessary for learning a foreign language by the method of working with native speakers and arriving inductively at the grammatical system of their language. An introduction to linguistic method.

BLOOMFIELD, LEONARD. *Outline Guide for the Practical Study of Foreign Languages*. Washington: Linguistic Society of America, 1942. Pp. 16.

A guide to learning a new language based on the linguistic scientists' approach; to be used with Bloch's and Traeger's *Outline of Linguistic Analysis*.

BOLLING, GEORGE M. "Acceleration of Language Teaching and the Classics," *Classical Philology*, XXXIX (April 1944), 101–6.

Discusses, among other things, what the classicists can do in language teaching, influenced by the so-called "Army method."

BOSSHARD, H. M. "The Speaking Approach to German at Clark University," *German Quarterly*, XIX (January 1946), 12–17.

Not a direct outcome of the ASTP, but is as much an outgrowth of *Basic German for Reading*, twice reported on previously by Bosshard.

BOTTKE, K. G., and MILLIGAN, E. E. "Test of Aural and Oral Aptitude for Foreign Language Study," *Modern Language Journal*, XXIX (December 1945), 705–9.

Test for oral production and aural comprehension, based on inference understanding, sound differentiation, assimilation and understanding of vocabulary in sentences, vowel timbre, work fluency, general hearing, ability to mimic, etc.

BRADY, THOMAS A., and STANKOWSKI, A. J. *The Foreign Area and Language Study at the University of Missouri. The University of Missouri Bulletin*, July 20, 1945, Vol. 46, No. 21, Arts and Science Series No. 2, Columbia, Mo.: University of Missouri, 1945. Pp. 160.

History of the establishment and operation of the Foreign Area and Language Program. Discusses staff, methods, screening, rating, materials used, and offers a critical evaluation of the program by both students and teachers.

BRANDT, THOMAS O. "War and Languages," *German Quarterly*, XVII (March 1944), 72–78.

Stresses development to greater extent of *Sprachgefuhl*. Analyzes language houses, radio, phonograph, and such devices in language learning.

BROWN, J. L. "Trends in Language Instruction," *Modern Language Journal*, XXVII (December 1943), 559–67.

Outlines the development of the oral approach through the informant, and shows that oral concentration in the early stages does not preclude the desirability of reading and writing later.

BROZEK, JOSEF. "Slavic Studies in America," *Journal of Higher Education*, XIV (June 1943), 293–96.

Statistics on the status of Slavic studies in America for 1941 and 1942. Supplements M. W. Rosenbaum's article in January 1943 issue.

BUENDIA, JORGE A. "Methods of Teaching Spanish at Yale University," *Hispania*, XXVII (May 1944), 178–208.

Description of the methods used in teaching Spanish at Yale.

BUSH, S. H., and COUSINS, C. E. "Foreign Language Classes in the University of Iowa," *Education*, LXV (May 1945), 558–61.

Program at Iowa is featured by giving an achievement test to students whenever they think they possess an adequate reading or speaking knowledge of the language from either high school or college work. After passing the achievement test, students continue in a special field such as language study, commercial aspects, literature, or speaking.

Bushnell, Marjorie R. "The Army Technique in the High School Class," *Modern Language Journal*, XXVIII (February 1944), 190–91.

Discusses ASTP features that can be utilized in the high school.

Carmody, Francis J. "ASTP Gives No Help to French Teachers," *California Journal of Secondary Education*, XX (May 1945), 257–62.

Written in disapproval of certain ASTP methods. Contains technical discussion of phonetics and phonemics. Trend in modern-language teaching is toward greater achievement in oral work; this should be encouraged but only to such degree as it serves the reading objective.

————. "Phonemic Theory and Practice Applied to the Teaching of French," *Modern Language Journal*, XXVIII (December 1944), 674–81.

This method may be all right for study of unusual languages, but is viewed as inefficient for the teaching of well-known languages.

Ceroni, Vittorio. "Three Months with the ASTP Teaching Italian," *Modern Language Journal*, XXVIII (January–February 1944) 46–49, 131–35.

Description of author's experiences in the ASTP teaching Italian. Numerous examples given to illustrate the methods used.

Clements, Robert J. "Leaving the Interpreters Behind," *Italica*, XXII (March 1945), 34–36.

Excerpts from letters of officers who had trained in the CATS at Harvard in Italian. Gives summaries of their experience with Italian in Italy.

Columbia University. "Announcement of the Russian Institute," *Columbia University Bulletin of Information*, 46th Series, No. 16. New York: March 1946.

Official Bulletin on Russian area study.

————. "Announcement of the School of International Affairs," *Columbia University Bulletin of Information*, 46th Series, No. 17. New York: March 1946.

Official college bulletin on new course of study, related to wartime area program.

Copley, Frank O. "The United States Armed Forces Institute," *Journal of the American Association of Collegiate Registrars*, XIX (April 1944), 287–94.

Relates to off-duty study of languages, among other subjects.

Corbato, Hermenegildo. "Experiences in the Teaching of Chinese," *California Journal of Secondary Education*, XX (May 1945), 250–56.

Explains how an intensive course in Chinese was organized and the results achieved, with some reasons for these.

Cowan, J. M., and Graves, M. "A Statement of Intensive Language Instruction," *German Quarterly*, XVII (November 1944), 165–66.

A series of eight statements as to *reasonable* expectations of results from the ASTP program. Considers some means of realizing them.

CROSS, EPHRAIM. "Honest Linguists, Racketeers, and the Innocent Public; Reply to W. Frauenfelder," *School and Society*, LX (October 28, 1944), 284–85.

An answer to a previous article in *School and Society*.

——. "Language Study and the Armed Forces," *Modern Language Journal*, XXVIII (March 1944), 292–95.

Critical study of what is new and old in language study; stresses the need for changes if the wartime program is to be adapted to peacetime.

CROSS, SAMUEL H. "On Teaching Contemporary Russian Civilization," *The Slavonic and East European Review*, XXII (1944), 93–101.

Examines this problem in the light of its past, present, and future possibilities. Conclusions not too positive.

——. "Reflections on the ASTP Language Program," *Education*, LXV (May 1945), 548–52.

Though the ASTP performed a useful function in wartime and made the public language-conscious, not all of the program can be adapted to the schools. Stresses the point that reading competence increases with speaking ability.

DEVANE, WILLIAM CLYDE. "American Education after the War," *Yale Review*, XXXIII (September 1943), 34–46.

Anent the formation of a common curriculum for general education.

DIEKHOFF, JOHN S. "The Mission and the Method of Army Language Teaching," *Bulletin of the American Association of University Professors*, XXXI (Winter 1945), 606–20.

Discusses the ASTP language program from the point of view of "different objectives," in contrast to the conventional; considers the "Army method" in the light of the "expedient method" and, with respect to Army materials, the "expedient content." Concludes with a section on academic adaptations.

DOYLE, HENRY GRATTAN. "Learning Languages in a Hurry—But Not by Miracles," *School and Society*, LVIII (December 18, 1943), 465–67.

Remarks on C. R. Walker's article "Language Teaching Goes to War," *School and Society* (April 3, 1943) and *Reader's Digest* (May 1943). The author stresses the point that while languages are being learned in a hurry, it is through long daily hours and hard constant drill—not by any magic method.

DUNKEL, HAROLD B. "The Investigation of the Teaching of a Second Language," *Modern Language Journal*, XXIX (April 1945), 323–25.

A brief sketch of the investigation of language teaching being conducted at the University of Chicago.

EATON, ESTHER M. "Can High School Modern Language Study Pay Dividends?" *Modern Language Journal*, XXX (January 1946), 20–26.

Describes the operation of an intensive program in foreign languages offered over an extended period in Garden City High School to show that many of the principles of the ASTP can be applied at the high school level.

ECKELBERRY, R. H. "Instruction in Modern Foreign Languages," *Journal of Higher Education*, XIV (June 1943), 312–14.

Report of a quick survey to determine the status of instruction in modern foreign languages, literatures, and cultures in American colleges and universities. Made in the belief that the war had created new demands for instruction in some areas and probably decreased in others.

ELDRIDGE, J. G. "Boom in Babel at Idaho," *School and Society*, LVII (November 13, 1943), 397–98.

Story of the ASTP at Idaho. Nine languages taught.

"Emphasis on Foreign Languages at Cornell University," *School and Society*, LVIII (October 30, 1943), 339–40.

Languages stressed at Cornell University in the regular classes as well as in the ASTP. Russian is now accepted among the prescribed languages satisfying the college language requirements for the A.B. degree.

ETMEKJIAN, JAMES. "Language Objectives of the Secondary Schools in the Postwar Period," *Modern Language Journal*, XXIX (October 1945), 477–80.

Selection of language and particular skill to be emphasized should depend upon the student's needs and interests. Discusses this problem from the view of three types of schools: commercial, general, and college preparatory.

FAUST, A. B. "A War-time Trend in Language Teaching," *German Quarterly*, XVII (March 1944), 93.

Expresses the point of view that a living foreign language is still universally expressed in the question, "Can you speak it?"

FAYER, MARGARET L. "Middlebury College and the Army Method of Teaching Languages," *School and Society*, LX (July 29, 1944), 79–80.

Takes a stand on "Army method" of language teaching, to point out what can and what cannot be adopted by civilian educators.

FEHLAU, ULAND E. "Cincinnati's New Language Course," *German Quarterly*, XIX (January 1946), 9–11.

Description of the new German course at the University of Cincinnati.

FENTON, WILLIAM N. "Area Studies in American Universities," *A Report on the Ethnogeographic Board Survey of the FAL Curricula of the ASTP and the CATS Programs in 1943–44*. Prepared for the Commission on Implications of Armed Services Educational Programs. In press.

A consolidated report of observations and visits to some twenty-five universities offering a foreign area and language program. Discusses areas and students, organization, integration, teaching methods, levels, and the impact of the program on the university. Contains a number of cases on relationship of curricular organization to subject-matter content.

———. *Reports on Area Studies in American Universities*. I, California (pp. 12); II, Chicago (pp. 36); III, Harvard (pp. 48); IV, Cornell (pp. 50); V, Carnegie Institute of Technology (pp. 5); VI, Grinnell (pp. 7). Washington: Ethnogeographic Board, Smithsonian Institution, 1945.

Objective reports on the area-study program to supplement the ASTP language survey for the Commission on Trends in Education of the Modern

Language Association. Investigates both the ASTP programs and the Civil Affairs Training Schools at the stated institutions.

FINE, BENJAMIN. "In 30 Tongues GI's Have a Word for It," *New York Times* Magazine (September 26, 1943), 16–17.

See also *New York Times* for November 19, 1944; for August 12, 1945; and for October 21, 1945.

"Foreign Languages and the Army Program," *School and Society*, LX (July 29, 1944), 78–79.

Describes ASTP program. Poi nts out that an extension of the prevailing conditions to regular foreign-language instruction would equip citizens for international contacts in a postwar world.

FRAUENFELDER, WILLIAM. "Lessons from Army Language Courses," *School and Society*, LX (August 19 , 1944), 123–24.

The ASTP course was too s hort-lived to be conclusive. Bard College will continue the experiment of the A STP in language and area work with civilian students who have a major inter est in linguistics.

FRAZIER, LEONARD G. *The Armed Forces Training Program of the University of California.* (Mimeographed.) Berkeley: University of California, President's Office, Berkeley, California, 1945. Pp. iv–95.

A partial survey of the activities on three of the eight campuses of the University in training members of the armed forces during the war years 1942–45.

FREEMAN, STEPHEN A. "Foreign Languages for Peace," *Journal of the American Association of Collegiate Registrars*, XX (April 1945), 293–312.

Brie f description of foreign-language instruction for the last thirty years, includi ng the ASTP. Points the challenge to teachers for peacetime l anguage teachin g that must include complete mastery of the language by the student.

FRENZ, HORST, and ITTNER, ROBERT T. "The German Area Course at Indiana University," *Indiana University News-Letter*, XXXIII (August 1945), 6.

Description of organization, content, methods of the area-study program in German.

FRIEDL, BERTHOLD C. "Techniques in Spoken Language: Specific Procedures in the ASTP Foreign Area and Language Studi es," *Modern Language Journal*, XXVIII (October 1944), 476–98.

A description of procedures used in the ASTP at the University of Missouri, with discussion of old and new techniques. Samples, especially of *comédies spontanées* are supplied.

FRIEDRICH, C. J. *School for Overseas Administration: Annual Report*, February 1943–February 1944. (Mimeographed.) Cambridge, Mass.: Harvard University, 1944. Pp. 32.

Established to serve the needs of civilian agencies of the government, but later, the needs of the armed services received central concern. Its purpose was to develop intensive programs of regional research and study for a few major areas.

FUERST, N. "Towards Defining the Intensive Course," *German Quarterly*, XVII (November 1944), 201–4.

Suggests the toleration of parallel differentiated methodologies and objectives.

FUNKE, ERICH. "Phonetics and Recent Developments in Language Study," *Modern Language Journal*, XXVII (October 1943), 419–25.

Discusses development of phonetics as an applied and experimental science, and also the value of phonetics training in the study of less-known languages.

———. "The Iowa Language Program," *German Quarterly*, XIX (January 1946), 29–32.

The new program in German influenced by the ASTP.

GALPIN, ALFRED. "Italian ASTP Program at the University of Wisconsin," *Italica*, XXI (March 1944), 25–28.

A description of the division of the course into *Mimica, Pratica*, and *Analisi*, discussing the content and methods of each.

GARDINER, CATHERINE A. "Oral Command the First Objective in Foreign Language Teaching," *School and Society*, LVIII (July 17, 1943), 43–44.

Plea for longer period of language study. Points out the fact that in many foreign countries, foreign-language study begins in preadolescence.

GHIGO, FRANCIS. "Standardized Tests in the ASTP at the University of North Carolina," *French Review*, XVII (May 1944), 358–60.

Analysis of results obtained through the use of standardized tests, each one given twice.

GIBSON, J. S. "Area-Language Training: An Army Experiment," *Education*, LXV (January 1945), 291–97.

A report on the ASTP and its objectives; asserts that there will be changes in the postwar period.

GIDUZ, HUGO. "On ASTP Language and Area Study," *French Review*, XVIII (December 1944), 129–31.

Describes the situation at Chapel Hill in the ASTP language and area program. Concludes with a few notes on possible adaptations.

GIRARD, DANIEL P. "The Teaching of Foreign Languages during and after the War," *French Review*, XVII (October 1943), 23–29.

The notion that we do not need foreign languages because English will soon be the universally used tongue is erroneous. Mutual understanding must be a two-way rather than a one-way process. Hearing, speaking, reading, and writing should be taught and in that order.

———. "Unit in Use of Audio-Visual Aids," *Modern Language Journal*, XXX (February 1946), 62–68.

Discusses audio-visual aids from the viewpoint of recent improvements, availability in the schools, and suggestions for their use.

GIRARD, DANIEL P. "The War, Foreign Languages, and the Schools of Tomorrow," *Teachers College Record*, XLV (April 1944), 471–77.

Author notes the inadequacy of instruction in foreign languages as they were taught before the war. Features that can be adapted from the wartime programs for school use are mentioned.

GOEDSCHE, C. R. "The Semi-Intensive Course at Northwestern," *German Quarterly*, XIX (January 1946), 42–47.

Describes the program and states that the revised two-year program has definite advantages over the traditional.

GORDON, LEWIS H. "Italian in the ASTP," *Italica*, XX (December 1943), 201–4.

A description of the methods and procedures used in Italian classes at Cornell. Students are carefully divided into sections on the basis of their abilities, background, spirit, application, etc.

GRAVES, MORTIMER. "A Memorandum on Regional Studies," *Journal of Higher Education*, XIV (November 1943), 431–34.

Stresses the importance of regional studies in the government's program of war and postwar education. Shows the Germans have moved somewhat farther than we have in having created a discipline known as *Nationenwissenschaft*. This includes two semesters' study of the language and script in question, followed by study in the history and culture of the people.

———. "War-time Instruction in Far Eastern Languages," *Far Eastern Survey*, XV (March 27, 1946), 92–93.

Discusses the activity and progress in the teaching of Far Eastern languages in the United States during the war.

GRAVES, MORTIMER, and COWAN, J. MILTON. *Report of the First Year's Operation of the Intensive Language Program of the American Council of Learned Societies*. Washington: American Council of Learned Societies, 1942. Pp. 40.

Defines intensive courses and methods. Contains a survey of the operations of the programs in the various languages.

GRISWOLD, A. WHITNEY. *Education for War and Reconstruction*. Issued by the Alumni Board of Yale University Press, June 1943. Pp. 16.

The program at Yale of foreign-area studies with an outline of lectures on "Italy and the Mediterranean."

HAAS, MARY R. "The Linguist as a Teacher of Languages," *Language*, XIX (July 1943), 203–8.

A discussion of the method of linguistic analysis as applied especially to the teaching of Oriental languages.

HALL, ROBERT A. "Progress and Reaction in Modern Language Teaching," *Bulletin of the American Association of University Professors*, XXX (Summer 1945), 220–30.

ASTP adopted the Intensive Language Program of the American Council of Learned Societies. The novel thing about the program is the combination of all the various features.

HALL, ROBERT A. "Some Desiderata for Elementary Language Texts," *Modern Language Journal*, XXIX (April 1945), 290–95.

An enumeration of certain features which appear desirable for elementary language texts in the light of recent improvements in approach and method.

HARRIS, JULIAN. "The 'Intensive' Method at Wisconsin," *French Review*, XVIII (May 1945), 338–49.

A description with samples and discussions of the beginning French courses at Wisconsin, with some results stated.

HARVARD UNIVERSITY. *Report of a Sub-Committee on Languages and International Affairs*, Faculty of Arts and Sciences, Committee on Education Policy, November 12, 1945. Pp. 27.

Proposal for a program of regional studies at Harvard, growing out of the war experience.

HARVITT, HÉLÈNE. "GI's Find French Useful," *French Review*, XVIII (March 1945), 278–81.

Extracts from letters of soldiers telling how their previous language training was of value to them in France.

HEINE-GELDERN, ROBERT. *A Survey of Studies on Southeast Asia at American Universities and Colleges*, East Indies Institute of America, New York, August 1943. Pp. 43.

Presents the questionnaire of the survey, an analysis of the replies, with conclusions and suggestions for a long-range program.

HERMAN, ABRAHAM. "Comments on the Survey of Language Classes in the ASTP," *Modern Language Journal*, XXIX (October 1945), 477–80.

Criticism of the survey of language classes in the ASTP.

HEWITT, THEODORE B. "The Place of German in the Post-War Curriculum," *Modern Language Journal*, XXIX (February 1945), 133–35.

Acceleration not altogether practical after relaxation of war pressure. Courses will need adjustment to meet requirements of returning veteran. Lack of opportunity for foreign study will promote our own summer language schools.

HITE, HILDA GRAY. "The Intersession Experiment at the University of Rochester," *German Quarterly*, XIX (January 1946), 72–75.

Language-house experiment for German during the summer session, and its advantages.

HOLZMANN, A. W. "A Report from Rutgers," *German Quarterly*, XIX (January 1946), News & Notes, 96.

Expansion of the offerings at a higher level rather than at the beginning of language study.

HUEBENER, THEODORE. "Letter to the Editor," *German Quarterly*, XVII (May 1944), 162–64.

Advocates more realistic curricular arrangements as indicated by the ASTP experiment.

HUEBENER, THEODORE. "What Shall the Aims of Foreign Language Teaching Be in the Light of Recent Experience?" *Modern Language Journal*, XXIX (May 1945), 411–13.

Greater stress can be given to oral activity, but since the greater part of the students taking language study will not continue with it after high school, the broader cultural and educational values must remain permanent.

HUTCHINSON, MARK E. "The War-time Language Program as Related to Post-war Language Teaching," *School and Society*, LX (July 15, 1944), 33–36.

A Latin teacher raises the question as to the validity of the "Army method" for the full language course.

———. "Foreign Languages in American Education," *School and Society*, LXII (September 8, 1945), 145–48.

Discusses some of the features of the ASTP that merit adoption in postwar education.

HYNEMAN, CHARLES S. "The Army's Civil Affairs Training Program," *American Political Science Review*, XXXVIII (April 1944), 342–53.

Discusses the complete program of the CATS; content, method, procedures, problems, teams, panels, etc.

———. "The War-time Area and Language Courses," *Bulletin of the American Association of University Professors*, XXXI (Autumn 1945), 434–47.

A report on the organization and objectives of the ASTP with remarks on adaptation of certain elements to civilian programs.

ITTNER, R. T. "Implications of the Armed Forces' Language Program," *German Quarterly*, XVII (November 1944), 176–82.

A study of the aural-oral approach in its relation to reading ability.

JOHNSON, LAURA B. "Some Implications of the Intensive Language Program for the Class Room Teacher," *French Review*, XVII (May 1944), 361–66.

Analyzes those features of the ASTP language courses which can be applied to regular high school classes.

JORDON, EMIL L. "An Experiment with ASTP Objectives in Second-Year German at Rutgers (N. J. C. for Women)," *German Quarterly*, XIX (January 1946), 76–80.

The project at Rutgers based on the ASTP for a second-year group, using long-tested college methods modified in the direction of real-life situations.

———. "Brazil: Foreign Area Studies in College Portuguese," *Modern Language Journal*, XXVIII (March 1944), 277–79.

Discusses the possibility of including Brazilian area studies in the Portuguese college teaching program.

———. "'Foreign Area Studies,' in the German College Curriculum," *Modern Language Journal*, XXVIII (February 1944), 151–54.

The author presents an outline of area study now in use at New Jersey College for Women resulting from the ASTP influence, and taken from a previous course called *Kulturgeschichte*. Outline is divided into two parts: The Country, and The People.

JORDON, EMIL L. "Spoken German: Methods and Results," *Modern Language Journal*, XXIX (January 1945), 48–54.

The need for experimentation is stressed in the field of methods in spoken German. Relative merits of imitation and intellectual initiative in oral training are discussed. Outlines a specific "short course" in spoken German to be given at the end of the elementary German course.

KARPOVA, SUZANNE V. "Six Months with the ASTP," *Journal of Higher Education*, XVI (February 1945), 63–69.

The author tells of the enthusiasm of the group of ASTP servicemen learning to speak Russian.

KAULFERS, WALTER V. "Grammar in and through Use," *Education*, LXV (May 1945), 562–70.

Advocates grammar teaching as a means of communication in action based on simple but interesting materials easily understood. Achievement should be judged on the basis of readiness to perform in situations related as closely as possible to real life.

———. "Instrumental Grammar for Conversation," *Modern Language Journal*, XXIX (February 1945), 99–111.

Discussion of the problem of teaching grammar for conversational use.

———. "Toward More Broadly Based Modern-Language Curricula," *School and Society*, LXII (December 1, 1945), 345–47.

Stresses the need for readjustment in certain phases of the organization and administration of postwar offerings in modern foreign languages at the college and university level.

———. "War-time Developments in Modern-Language Achievement Testing," *Modern Language Journal*, XXVIII (February 1944), 136–50.

Discusses the theory and practice of aural-comprehension and oral-fluency testing, illustrated with examples in point.

KLARMAN, A. D. "The Challenge of the Army," *German Quarterly*, XVII (March 1944), 67–71.

Suggests ways and means of adapting curricular arrangements to civilian institutions by condensing the language course into one year of six, seven, or more hours per week. Laboratory periods with language drill would supplement more formal instruction.

KURATH, HANS. "Report on the Demonstration Class in Elementary German Sponsored by the Linguistic Institute of the Linguistic Society of America at the University of Michigan in the Summer of 1945," *German Quarterly*, XIX (January 1946), 33–35.

Contains a supplementary report by Professor W. F. Striedieck. Shows the value of concentrated hours of study.

LA DU, MILAN S. "Army Language Instruction at Syracuse University," *Modern Language Journal*, XXVIII (March 1944), 286–88.

Tells the principal aspects of the ASTP language program at Syracuse. Describes the aims, materials, methods, segregation by competence, etc.

LANGELLIER, PAUL. "Un recensement d'opinions sur les cours 'intensifs'," *French Review*, XVIII (March 1945), 274–77.

Summary of the results of a questionnaire sent to institutions which have already set up an "intensive" program.

LEAVITT, STURGIS. "Why Waste Time? Report on the Preliminary Spanish Program, University of North Carolina," *Hispania*, XXVI (October 1943), 310–11.

The author describes the intensive Spanish program set up to accommodate the trainees of the ASTP units before the beginning of the actual work.

LEONARD, IRVING A. "A Survey of Personnel and Activities in Latin American Aspects of the Humanities and Social Sciences at Twenty Universities of the United States," *Joint Committee on Latin American Studies*, No. 1, April 1943. Pp. 59.

Survey, jointly sponsored by National Research Council, American Council of Learned Societies, and the Social Science Research Council.

LEVY, BERNARD. "Foreign Language Teaching Aims and Methods in the Light of the ASTP," *Modern Language Journal*, XXIX (May 1945), 403–10.

Believes that through the aural-oral approach reading ability can be established. Colloquial conversation models must be used, and grammar taught inductively. Little writing and no insistence on spelling in the early stages. Reading as such should be undertaken in the final year of language study.

LINDQUIST, LILLY. "Why Study Foreign Languages Answered by Our Armed Forces," *Modern Language Journal*, XXVIII (March 1944), 289–91.

A plea for a wider application of oral procedures in the schools for building an elementary speaking knowledge first, as a basis for later, more thorough knowledge.

MEESSEN, H. J. "The Aural-Oral Sections at the University of Minnesota, 1944–45," *German Quarterly*, XIX (January 1946), 36–41.

Experiment which concludes that the aural-oral method is justified as an approach to language study. This method may become a valid method for perhaps half the language students.

METCALF, GEORGE J. "Experiments with Intensive Language Teaching at the University of Chicago," *German Quarterly*, XIX (January 1946) 6–8.

Discusses two innovations at Chicago—a general course in language as a degree requirement for all college students and the intensive twelve-week summer course in elementary German of twelve contact hours a week.

MEYER, WILLIAM G. "Nutley High School's Plan of Language Teaching," *German Quarterly*, XVIII (November 1945), 172–75.

Describes the plan of limiting classes in foreign-language study to fifteen students and requiring four years' work accomplished in two years by daily double-period sessions.

MICHAEL, FRANZ H. "Civilians and Soldiers Study Pacific," *Far Eastern Survey*, XIII (August 23, 1944).

Brief story of the ASTP foreign area and language program at the University of Washington and mention of establishment of a program of Far Eastern study utilizing the new Army technique.

MILLER, V. D. "ASTP Influence on Modern Language Teaching," *California Journal of Secondary Education*, XX (May 1945), 263–70.

Considers the way in which secondary-school language instruction can be improved as a result of the Army's intensive program, by suggesting improvements that are indicated as a result of the Army's successes and failures.

MILLIGAN, E. E. "Trial Balance Sheet," *Modern Language Journal*, XXIX (February 1945), 112–16.

Evaluation of the writer's experience in teaching in the ASTP. Describes what is to be avoided and what should be included in the postwar civilian programs.

MOORE, OLIN H. "G. I. 'Italo-Americani nell' ASTP," *Italica*, XXI (September 1944), 125–30.

Discussion of problems of adjustment faced in an advanced class of ASTP made up of Italo-Americans.

MORGAN, B. Q. "After the War; A Blueprint for Action," *Modern Language Journal*, XXVIII (April 1944), 323–24.

A plea for effective action in language teaching, stressing the promotion of public relations as well as effort toward improvement in teaching.

———. "An Experiment at Stanford University," *German Quarterly*, XIX (January 1946), News & Notes, 96–97.

A brief note on an inconclusive experiment in teaching German.

———. "A Memorandum on the 'Intensive' Course in a Foreign Language," *German Quarterly*, (November 1943), 199–201.

A discussion of the meaning of "intensive" with a brief consideration of the various factors in such courses. Contains also specific suggestions for aural-oral practice.

———. "Reflections of the 'Intensive' Course in Foreign Language," *Modern Language Journal*, XXVII (December 1944), 568–70.

Old and new features of the Army language courses and drawbacks to such a course are discussed.

———. "Teachers' Opinions of the Army Method," *California Journal of Secondary Education*, XX (May 1945), 271–76.

Data on the results of a questionnaire sent out to secondary-school language teachers in California on what is now being done or contemplated with respect to adoption of Army intensive methods on the secondary level.

MORRISON, J. CAYCE. "An Administrator Looks at Language Study," *Modern Language Journal*, XXIX (December 1945), 679–87.

Discusses past and future of language study. The ASTP in the language program has raised many questions which must be finally answered in terms of experimentation and research. This may mean reorganization of the school curriculum or the school day.

MOSES, B. HOPKINS. "Methods of 'Learning in a Hurry': Their Contribution to Education," *School and Society*, LIX (May 13, 1944), 348–49.

The author finds an important contribution to educational methods in the intensive concentration of a limited number of courses for a short time as exemplified by ASTP language and area work.

MYRON, HERBERT B. "Languages Anew," *Modern Language Journal*, XXX (March 1946), 122–33.

Attempts, in the light of recent educational trends, to bring new classifications to the problems of language study and teaching. Discusses aims, objectives, methods, subject matter, and administrative and curricular policy.

———. "Teaching French to the Army," *French Review*, XVII (May 1944), 345–52.

A description of Army work in French using a hypothetical class as a sample of the type of work done. Contains some suggestions for adaptation to civilian language work.

"New Courses on Far Eastern Areas and Languages at Stanford," *School and Society*, LXI (May 19, 1945), 325.

Grants made by Rockefeller Foundation for visiting lecturers and, after the war, for travel and study in the Far East. The program has as its objective to give the student a broad over-all understanding of the geography, peoples, history, politics, religions, and cultures of the Pacific-Asiatic-Russian regions in addition to a more intimate acquaintance and language facility with a specific country or area.

NEW YORK UNIVERSITY, BUREAU OF INFORMATION. "Army Methods of Teaching Foreign Languages," *Monatshefte für Deutschen Unterricht*, XXXVI (February 1944), 109–10.

A statement of the changes needed in college curricula before Army methods of teaching languages can be adopted.

NICHOLSON, HELEN S. "Learning by the Linguist-Informant Method," *Modern Language Journal*, XXVIII (November 1944), 615–19.

A review of the personal experience of the author in attending classes in Malay conducted in accordance with the linguist-informant method.

NORDMEYER, GEORGE, and WHITE, JAMES F. "Intensive German at Yale," *German Quarterly*, XIX (January 1946), 86–94.

Describes the program in German at Yale, where both the traditional and the intensive courses are offered. It is believed that offering both types of courses provides the best opportunity for each student to develop himself.

NORDSIECK, REINHOLD. "A Brief Report on Intensive, Semi-Intensive, and Special Courses in German at the Ohio State University," *German Quarterly*, XIX (January 1946), 48–51.

Describes briefly old and new types of "intensive" courses at the university.

OELLRICH, PAULA. "Reaction of High School Language Teachers to 'New' Methods," *French Review*, XIX (October 1945), 37–41.

A survey of opinion based on a questionnaire sent to selected high school language teachers throughout the country.

OLINGER, H. C. "Whither Foreign Languages?" *Modern Language Journal*, XXIX (December 1945), 665–70.

One of a series of replies to a questionnaire submitted by the *Modern Language Journal* in surveying the influence of the war and the ASTP on language study. Series continues in Vol. XXX.

PARGMENT, M. S. "On Learning a Foreign Language," *Modern Language Journal*, XXIX (March 1945), 198–209.

Though the ASTP gave the impression that languages can be taught quickly, there is no short cut to learning a foreign language. For improvement in teaching it will be necessary to have competent teachers, longer periods of instruction, smaller classes, and lighter teaching loads.

———. "Preparation of College Teachers in Modern Foreign Languages," *The Educational Record*, XXV (January 1944), 75–86.

Certain definite skills can be imparted that will satisfy the students and the public. These skills are a reading knowledge of material of average difficulty and the ability, within certain limits, to understand the spoken language and use it orally and in writing. The teacher should leave with his students an acquaintance with the civilization and the contemporary culture of the country whose language he teaches.

———. "What Constitutes a Reading Knowledge of a Foreign Language, and How it can be Acquired," *French Review*, XVII (December 1943), 74–82.

Examines what is meant by a reading knowledge and the conditions necessary to attain it.

PAULSEN, W. "The ASTP Experiment and Our Future Language Courses," *German Quarterly*, XVII (November 1944), 167–75.

Stresses the need for clarification of tasks and objectives.

PEI, MARIO A. "A Letter to Fortune," *Bulletin of the New England Modern Language Association*, VI, November–December.

———. "Science Comes to Language: A Reply," *Fortune*, XXX (December 1944), 278.

An answer to the article appearing in *Fortune*, August 1944. Weaknesses and misinterpretations are pointed out.

———. "A Modern Language Teacher Replies," *Bulletin of the American Association of University Professors*, XXXI (Autumn 1945), 409–17.

An answer to Professor Hall's article on "Progress and Reaction in Modern Language Teaching."

PEISEL, HERBERT H. J. "Audiatur et Altera Pars: A Report from the University of Pennsylvania," *German Quarterly*, XIX (January 1946), 52–64.

Discusses aims, procedures, results, and conclusions on the experiment in German.

PEYTON, MYRON S. "A Note on Present Attitudes toward Foreign-Language Teaching," *Modern Language Journal*, XXIX (November 1945), 596–602.

Discusses the place of foreign languages today as an aftermath of the wartime experiences.

PITCHER, STEPHEN L. "Application of ASTP Experiences to Language Teaching in Secondary and Elementary Schools," *Hispania*, XXIX (May 1946), 190–96.

Discusses and analyzes the ASTP features applicable to the secondary level.

———. "The Teaching of Spanish and Portuguese." For the National Education Association of the United States, 1201 16th Street, N. W., Washington, August 1945. Pp. 23.

A report on a series of regional conferences sponsored by the National Education Association and conducted in cooperation with the Office of Inter-American Affairs. Contains summaries of a few addresses.

PITTSBURGH, UNIVERSITY OF. "Area and Language Studies," *Bulletin of the University of Pittsburgh*, (Fall Semester, 1945–46), p. 6.

Explanation and listing of courses for Latin America, China and the Far East, Russia, Germany, and France.

POLINGER, ELLIOT H. "Some Solutions of the Modern Language Problem," *Hispania*, XXVIII (November 1945), 532–39.

Discusses ways and means of adapting intensive methods to schools and colleges as a result of experience in the ASTP.

PRAGER, FRANKLIN. "A Defense of Army-Education Technique as Applied to Foreign Language," *School and Society*, LXI (January 27, 1945), 58–59.

For the masses to be taught foreign languages for the purpose of social intercourse and appreciation, the military stress on conversation rather than literature is by far the more practical and effective.

PRICE, MAURICE T. "A Proposal for Foreign-Area Courses," *Bulletin of the American Association of University Professors*, XXXI (Winter 1945), 648–67.

An attempt to think of area study in the light of socio-cultural regions, or sets of people. Discusses the institutions of higher learning equipped to provide a moderate concentration of curricular courses on one or more of these regions. Treats minimum personnel, subject matter, and requirements.

REHDER, H., and TWADDELL, W. F. "ASTP at Wisconsin," *German Quarterly*, XVII (November 1944), 216–23.

Points out the chief distinction of the work reported, with modifications of Bloomfield's general suggestions and Army directives.

———. "The Conversational Approach at the University of Wisconsin," *German Quarterly*, XIX (January 1946), 81–85.

The experiment at Wisconsin, dealing with history and organization, objective, method, reading, examinations, and general impressions.

REICHENBERGER, ARNOLD G. "Report on the Teaching of Beginning Italian in the ASTP at the Ohio State University, 1943–1944," Part I, *Modern Language Journal*, XXX (February 1946), 89–97. Part II, *Modern Language Journal*, XXX (March 1946), 137–44.

"A Report on Foreign Languages," *School and Society*, LX (September 9, 1944), 167–68.

A report on some of the language programs offered in universities for the year 1944.

RICE, WINTHROP H., and BOGDEN, HELEN. "Teaching Foreign Languages," *Review of Educational Research*, XVI (April 1946), 139–60.

Discusses the foreign-language teaching situation including a section on the ASTP methods, followed by a bibliography of the period covered.

ROCKEFELLER FOUNDATION, HUMANITIES DIVISION. *A Review of Far Eastern and Slavic Studies in Five Institutions of the Western States.* (Mimeographed.) (1944). Pp. 40.

Notes on the conference by David H. Stevens. General information on the Eastern and Slavic studies of the University of Washington, University of California, Stanford, Pomona, University of Colorado. First eight pages contain a general summary.

———. *Conference on Area and Language Programs in American Universities, Philadelphia.* (Mimeographed.) Pp. 147+5 app.

Roundtable discussion presided over by Mortimer Graves, with representatives from the War Department, the Smithsonian Institution, and several universities.

ROGERS, PAUL P. "Lessons from the ASTP of Language Teaching for Normal Times," *Hispania*, XXVII (February 1945), 44–49.

Discusses features adaptable to civilian education. Points out that needs of the Army were specific and for a definite moment.

ROSE, ERNST. "The Future of the ASTP Program," *German Quarterly*, XVII (May 1944), 161–62.

Discusses features of the ASTP adaptable to the secondary level, and their use.

ROWE, BENJAMIN. "The Army Streamlines Language Instruction," *Modern Language Journal*, XXIX (February 1945), 136–41.

Observations of a soldier-student in language study, especially Spanish.

RYDEN, EINAR R. "The G. I. Looks at the ASTP," *Modern Language Journal*, XXIX (October 1945), 498–502.

Questionnaire administered to eighty-one trainees of the ASTP reveals that the majority approve the intensive courses.

SANDRI, LUIGI, and KAULFERS, WALTER V. "An Oral-Fluency Rating Scale in Italian," *Italica*, XXII (September 1945), 133–44.

An individual test which attempts to measure readiness to perform in real-life situations.

SCANIO, VINCENT A. "The Army Intensive Language Program," *Michigan Alumnus Quarterly Review*, L (July 1944), 362–67.

The author was senior instructor for nine months in Italian at University of Michigan. Describes distinctive features of the ASTP and states requirements of students in the nine months' course.

————. "Some Lessons Learned from the Army Intensive Language Program," *Italica*, XXI (December 1944), 186–95.

The ASTP is full of potential significance to the future of foreign-language teaching in America. After his nine months' experience, author believes that valuable lessons have been learned.

SCHAEFFER, RUDOLF F. "The Peace-time Value of Army Language Training to the Trainee," *School and Society*, LIX (May 13, 1944), 346–48.

Describes the oral approach through the "mimi-memo" method which does not exclude grammar but uses it functionally.

SCHERER, G. A. C. "The Military German Course," *Monatshefte für Deutschen Unterricht*, XXXII (October 1943), 338–42.

An analysis and digest of replies to a questionnaire on courses in military German. Not ASTP; a two- or three-credit course. Lists texts.

————. "A New College Language Course for Beginners," *Modern Language Journal*, XXIX (October 1945), 503–8.

Suggestions for setting up classes in peacetime similar to the ASTP.

SCHMERTZING, WOLFGANG VON. "What Should be the Function of the Informant?" *Monatshefte für Deutschen Unterricht*, XXXVI (October 1944), 304–8.

Analyzes specific "should's" as to the personality, function, and technique of informants.

SCHOLZ, ALBERT. "A Method of Teaching Modern Languages," *Modern Language Journal*, XXIX (December 1945), 688–92.

Suggestions for classroom procedure are made. Points out also that the language is best learned through the ear.

SCHUELER, H. "Foreign Language Teaching under the Army Specialized Training Program," *German Quarterly*, XVII (November 1944), 183–91.

Summarizes and evaluates work done at Queens College during the war.

"Science Comes to Language," *Fortune*, XXX (August 1944), 133–35, 236–40.

This article deals with the approach to language teaching according to the method of the linguistic-scientist and contains a brief word about Franz Boas, founder of the American linguistic school.

SEBEOK, THOMAS A. "Linguist, Informant, and Units," *Modern Language Journal*, XXIX (May 1945), 376–81.

Discusses personal experience with Hungarian and Finnish.

SHELTON, WHITFORD H. "The Intensive Method at the University of Pittsburgh," *German Quarterly*, XIX (January 1946), 65–69.

Discusses the language program generally at Pittsburgh and the changes effected as a result of experiments.

SIMMONS, ERNEST J. "Intensive Study of Contemporary Russian Civilization," Final Report. (Mimeographed.) Ithaca, N. Y.: Cornell University,
1943. Pp. 104.
> History of the summer program at Cornell University. No language
offered. Concurrent courses on history, government, economic life, social
institutions, literature, and the weekly workshops. Contains list of materials
used, course outline, tests, and a summary of evaluation of the program by
the students.

————. "Study of Contemporary Russian Civilization," *Journal of Higher
Education*, XIV (November 1943), 439–40.
> Discusses the need for our educational practice to become international
in scope. Describes briefly the experiment on Russian civilization at Cornell.

SIMPSON, LURLINE V. "Linguistic Blitz," *Modern Language Journal*, XXIX
(May 1945), 382–85.
> Points out that language teachers should profit by the interest in foreign
languages by reaction to the Army courses. They should reconsider aims
and revitalize methods.

SKINNER, LAWRENCE HENRY. "The Role of Modern Foreign Languages in
Post-War Education," *Journal of the American Association of Collegiate
Registrars*, XIX (October 1943), 27–37.
> Presents a discussion on future position after giving a brief historical
sketch of language teaching. Stress is made on language use on a broad
scale, cultural as well as practical.

SOKOL, A. E. "The Army Language Program," *Journal of Higher Education*,
XVII (January 1946), 9–16.
> Discusses the language program from the viewpoint of lessons to be
learned for postwar education.

SONTAG, RAYMOND J. "The Significance of Area Studies for the Reconstruction of the College Curriculum," *Fall Meeting, Western College Association*,
(November 13, 1943), University of California, Berkeley, California. [Ad-
dresses on Wartime Problems of Higher Education.]
> Stresses the need for integration of disciplines in area study programs for
success.

SPRINGER, OTTO. "Intensive Language Study as a Part of the College Curriculum," *German Quarterly*, XVII (November 1944), 224–40.
> Indicates in detail practical measures for incorporating intensive language
training in the college curriculum.

STARCK, TAYLOR. "A Report from Harvard," *German Quarterly*, XIX (January 1946), News & Notes, 95–96.
> Brief sketch of experimental programs at Harvard, especially the summer
term of ten weeks.

STROEBE, LILIAN L. "Once More—Intensive Course in Foreign Languages,"
Monatshefte für Deutschen Unterricht, XXXVI (October 1944), 309–13.
> Discusses the pedagogic unsoundness of intensification and acceleration.
Makes practical suggestions as to use of curricular time allowance.

STURTEVANT, EDGAR H. "What Is a Linguist?" *Modern Language Journal,* XXVII (November 1944), 608–14.

A definition of the special meaning of "linguist" or "linguistic scientist," by an expert in the field.

Survey of Language Classes in the Army Specialized Training Program. Report of a Special Committee, prepared for the Commission on Trends in Education of the Modern Language Association. New York: Modern Language Association, 1944. Pp. 34.

An extensive analysis of the organization, aims, methods, and results of the ASTP in language study, with a summary of opinions, conclusions, and recommendations.

TAPPIN, CLARENCE L. "Where Do We Go from Here?" *Bulletin of the New England Modern Language Association,* VI (November–December 1944), 9–11.

A high school teacher views with some alarm the emphasis on intensive courses rejecting reading aims. Seeks a middle ground.

"Tests Now Available through the Investigation of the Teaching of a Second Language," *Modern Language Journal,* XXIX (November 1945), 633–34.

Description of aural-oral tests.

THOMAS, LAWRENCE G. "Can the Social Sciences Learn from the Army Program?" *Journal of Higher Education,* XVII (January 1946), 17–25.

After two years' experience working in the Army's training programs established at Stanford during the war, the author is concerned with the significance of the ASTP and the CATS programs for university instruction of civilian students in peacetime.

ULMER, BERNHARD. "The Intensive Course at Princeton," *German Quarterly,* XIX (January 1946), 70–71.

Discusses recent changes in German courses, methods, procedures, hours, etc.

UNITED STATES WAR DEPARTMENT. *United States Army and Navy Manual of Military Government and Civil Affairs.* Field Manual FM 27–5. (Restricted.) Washington: Government Printing Office, December 1943. Pp. 86.

Manual for civil affairs officers to be used as a suggestive guide in the handling of problems to be encountered.

VAETH, J. GORDON. "Language Study by Naval Personnel in Latin America," *Hispania,* XXVIII (February 1945), 94–97.

Discusses courses offered through the Armed Forces Institute for off-duty instruction.

VAIL, C. C. D. "The Rockefeller Language Conference," *German Quarterly,* XVII (May 1944), 120–30.

A résumé of the mimeographed report published at the conclusion of the conference. Provides stimulating opinions on: (1) intensive courses in college; (2) reading knowledge as the chief objective; (3) relationship of speaking knowledge to reading knowledge; (4) the place of phonetics and grammar in the scheme of instruction; (5) college language requirements; (6) the use of informants; (7) mechanical devices and dictionaries; and (8) implementation. Stresses the need of a greater degree of coordination and cooperation between language and the social studies.

VAIL, C. C. D. "State Requirements for Language Teachers," *Modern Language Journal.* XXIX (October 1945), 509–16.

A study of certification requirements for language teachers as of 1942. Until these requirements meet the needs of an aural-oral objective, the so-called "Army method" cannot be universally adopted in the high schools.

VON HOFE, HAROLD. "Intensive Language Study at the University of Southern California," *School and Society*, LXIII (November 27, 1943), 430–31.

Describes the intensive courses which were taught during a five-week intersession in French, German, and Spanish.

WAHLGREN, ERIK. "Area-language German: A Retrospective Commentary," *Modern Language Forum*, XXIX (June-September 1944), 69–84.

Describes personal experiences and methods used in ASTP German.

WALLACE, SCHUYLER C. "The Navy School of Military Government and Administration," *Annals of the American Academy of Political and Social Science*, CCXXXI (January 1944), 29–33.

History and exposition of the school at Columbia. Contains some implications for postwar education.

"War Courses at Yale, French (Foreign Area Studies)," *French Review*, XVII (October 1943), 49–50.

WAXMAN, SAMUEL M. "Foreign Languages and the U.S. Army," *Education*, LXV (May 1945), 553–57.

Discusses the ASTP at Boston University.

WENDT, PAUL. "Post-War Implications for Education in the Audio-Visual Programs of Our Armed Services," *Educational Screen*, XXIII (April 1944), 153–56.

In the planning and utilization of audio-visual aids and in the invention of new devices, the armed services have made a unique contribution to audio-visual education in this country.

WHITE, EMILIE M. "Foreign Languages—for War and Peace," *Journal of the National Education Association*, XXXIII (February 1944), 49.

The war has given a new importance to the teaching of foreign languages. Describes the methods used in the ASTP; eighteen life situations of a routine or emergency character are outlined.

———. "A Plea for Understanding," *School and Society*, LXII (November 24, 1945), 339–40.

The curve of forgetting is operative in all subjects to which continuing attention is not given. The public and educational administrators should lend a sympathetic ear to the plea for an earlier beginning and a longer period of language study.

WHITEHOUSE, ROBERT S. "The Workshop Program: Demonstrating the Value of the Language Laboratory," *Modern Language Journal*, XXIX (November 1945), 590–95.

A language workshop established to aid students in development of the oral skills.

WILLEY, MALCOLM M. "The College Training Programs of the Armed Services,"*Annals of the American Academy of Political and Social Science*, CCXXXI (January 1944), 14–28.

General survey of all the programs in colleges and universities sponsored by the Army and Navy.

WITHERS, A. M. "War on 'Language Teaching Goes to War,'" *School and Society*, LVIII (October 30, 1943), 346–48, and *Hispania*, XXVII (February 1944), 70–71.

A reply to the article "Language Teaching Goes to War," (*School and Society*, April 3, 1943).

WOOLEY, E. O. "Anent Conversational German," *Monatshefte für Deutschen Unterricht*, XXXVII (February 1945), 113–15.

Review of *Conversational German*, by Rehder & Twaddell (Henry Holt and Co.).

ZECH, ADOLPH. "Appraisal and Presentation of an Intensive Course in German," *Modern Language Journal*, XXIX (January 1945), 18–25.

The urgent need for oral-aural language teaching deserves attention. The experiments of the ASTP had good and bad features. Points out that the reading method and the oral-aural method cannot be combined into one method.

ZEYDEL, EDWIN H. "The ASTP Courses in Area and Language Study," *Modern Language Journal*, XXVII (November 1943), 459.

The editor of the *Journal* calls attention to the new courses and their importance to the future of these studies.

ARMY AND NAVY DOCUMENTS[1]

UNITED STATES NAVY DEPARTMENT. OFFICE OF THE CHIEF OF NAVAL OPERATIONS. "Military Government." On file in History Division, Office of Naval History, Navy Department. 3 vols.

———. "School of Oriental Languages." On file in History Division, Office of Naval History, Navy Department. 1 vol.

UNITED STATES WAR DEPARTMENT. "The Training History of the Military Intelligence Service Language School." On file in Historical Division, War Department Special Staff. Pp. 37; 15 annexes as follows:

    1. Academic Training History. Pp. 103.
    2. Administrative Section History. Pp. 10 + addenda.
    3. The Army Japanese Language School. Pp. 160.
    4. Intelligence Section History. Pp. 35 + addenda.

---

[1] Drafts in typewritten or mimeographed form.

5. The Chinese Section. Pp. 3.
6. JOB, Research and Field Liaison Office, Catalog of Captured Japanese Documents, etc.
7. The Korean Division. Pp. 4.
8. Library and Supply Section. Pp. 19.
9. Personnel Office. Pp. 46 + addenda.
10. Personnel Procurement Office, Procurement of Students, and Teachers (pages unnumbered).
11. Radio Section. Pp. 6.
12. Special Service Office. Pp. 14.
13. Translation Section. Pp. 47.
14. WAC Detachment. Pp. 2.
15. *a*) Legal Assistance. Pp. 6.
    b) Military Training. Pp. 6.

———. "History of Training, Military Government." On file in Historical Division, War Department Special Staff. Pp. 118.

———. "A History of the Army Specialized Training Program" (from its beginning to 31 December 1944). On file in Historical Division, War Department Special Staff. Pp. 191.

———. "History of Training, Army Specialized Training Program" (1 January 1945–30 June 1945). On file in Historical Division, War Department Special Staff. Pp. 35.

YAMAGIWA, JOSEPH K. "Japanese Language Programs, University of Michigan, World War II." (Mimeographed.) Ann Arbor, Mich., 1946. 5 vols. On file in Historical Division, War Department Special Staff.

THE AMERICAN COUNCIL ON EDUCATION

GEORGE F. ZOOK, *President*

A. J. BRUMBAUGH, *Vice President*

The American Council on Education is a *council* of national educational associations; organizations having related interests; approved universities, colleges, and technological schools; state departments of education; city school systems; selected private secondary schools; and selected educational departments of business and industrial companies. It is a center of co-operation and coordination whose influence has been apparent in the shaping of American educational policies as well as in the formulation of American educational practices during the past twenty-eight years. Many leaders in American education and public life serve on the commissions and committees through which the Council operates.

The Commission on Implications of Armed Services Educational Programs began its work in July 1945. It undertakes to identify features of the wartime training and educational programs worthy of adaptation and experimentation in peacetime civilian education of any and all types and levels. It also undertakes to make available to the public well-considered answers to the questions: What should education in America gain from the experience of the vast wartime training efforts? What are the implications for education and the national culture and strength, now and in the future?